THE STORY OF AMERICAN AVIATION

WITH ILLUSTRATIONS

"The thrilling story of how the airplane grew and the part it has played in the war and peace-time history of the United States of America."

JIM RAY

Published by

Hawk Press
4836/24, Ansari Road, Daryaganj
New Delhi – 110 002
Phones: 91-11-23278618, 91-11-43667199
e-mail: thehawkpress@gmail.com
www.jeevansonspublications.com

ISBN:978-93-88318-37-2

FOREWORD

In the following pages, Jim Ray, talented in his work of presentation and a conscientious student of aviation, presents a chain of highlights in the progress of American aëronautics. The work as a whole is directed toward a sound conception of the steps which have been taken in aircraft development. In so far as possible, without being exhaustive, Mr. Ray has portrayed the engineering advancement which underlies the structure of our swiftly developing air age. The reader who thoroughly digests the text and illustrations of this book will find that it is an orderly and faithful guide.

GILL ROBB WILSON

Aviation Editor,
New York Herald Tribune
Director of Aviation
State of New Jersey

INTRODUCTION

It is difficult to believe that, just a little over thirty years ago, I was a high-school student watching the pilots at the Wright Brothers' exhibition of the world's first flying machine. That machine weighed about eight hundred pounds. Its engine developed thirty horsepower. It flew at the then astounding speed of forty-two miles an hour, which is equal to the landing speed of our slowest light plane today. High-school students now are accustomed to the sight of giant airplanes whose weight is measured in tons and whose horsepower mounts to the thousands.

December, 1945, marks the forty-second anniversary of the first flight of an airplane. The progress of aviation since that first flight still seems unbelievable, even to one who has followed its development closely. The purpose of this book is to trace the progress of aviation in America and to tell the story of the men and machines that have given this country supremacy in the air.

In telling the story of American aviation from Kitty Hawk to the present day, I have been able to touch only the high spots in its dramatic progress. Space limitations prevent me from giving personal credit to the hundreds of pioneer airmen, engineers, and mechanics who have contributed so greatly to the progress of American aviation. Lack of space also makes it impossible to give the complete story of the great Government research organization, the National Advisory Committee for Aëronautics, whose work has been most fruitful in the advancement of civil and military aëronautics in the United States.

As we look over the record of the astounding progress of American aviation in forty-two years, let us salute our military leaders who have visualized the need for air power; the men who have designed and built our great engines and airplanes, and the leaders of commercial aviation who have made air travel fast, safe, and economical.

JIM RAY

Ottsville, Pennsylvania,
1945

CONTENTS

1

THE BEGINNINGS OF AMERICAN AVIATION

THE FLIGHT OF ETANA

THE DREAMERS

The idea of human flight has excited man's imagination for thousands of years. From stories and legends handed down through the years, we know that even from earliest times people dreamed of flying. There are visions of conquering the air in the colorful legends of winged men and beasts found in ancient folklore. The winged statuary of the Egyptians was no doubt inspired by the desire to imitate the flight of birds. In Greek mythology Hermes, the messenger of the gods, is clothed with winged sandals and helmet.

Historians have unearthed stories in cuneiform writing of man's attempts to fly. Some of these inscriptions date back more than five thousand years, to 3500 B.C. Perhaps the most famous of these stories is the ancient Babylonian tale of the shepherd boy, Etana, who rode on the back of an eagle.

The story of Dædalus and Icarus also tells us that man believed flying was somehow possible. Dædalus was a very clever man who lived with his son Icarus on the Island of Crete. The king of this island requested Dædalus to build a labyrinth or maze for him. Dædalus constructed the labyrinth so cleverly that only the king, who had the clue to the winding passages, could find his way out. One day the king became very angry at Dædalus and threw both him and his son Icarus into the labyrinth, intending that they should perish. Dædalus, who had been dreaming of flying, fashioned wings from wax and feathers, with which he and Icarus could fly to freedom. He cautioned Icarus that he must not fly too high or the sun would melt the wax in his wings. Icarus, impatient to escape, scarcely listened. Like birds the two flew into the air, quickly leaving the walls of the labyrinth. Dædalus, flying low, safely crossed the sea and reached Sicily. Icarus, unfortunately, failed to heed his father's warning. Flying was so much fun that he rose higher and higher. Suddenly feathers began to drop one by one. Too late Icarus realized that the sun had melted the wax in his wings. Down, down he fell into the sea.

Another ancient myth of flying concerns Pegasus, the winged horse. Bellerophon, a Corinthian hero, rode Pegasus and with his help killed a horrible monster called the Chimera.

Not only did men of long ago dream of flying—some of them firmly believed it could be done. Archimedes, a great Greek mathematician born in 287 B.C., was one. In the year 1250 an Englishman, Roger Bacon, had the idea that a large hollow globe of thin metal could be made which, when filled with an ethereal air or liquid fire, would float on the air like a ship on water.

Leonardo da Vinci, the great Italian artist and scientist, who lived in the fifteenth century, spent years experimenting with the idea of flying. He made a number of sketches of wings to be fitted to the arms and legs of man. His plan for a parachute was soundly worked out and his idea that the wings of a flying machine should be patterned after the wings of the bat found expression in the doped fabric covering of our early airplanes.

Aviation today is such an accepted fact that we sometimes forget how men from different parts of the world had to work, suffer hardships, face ridicule, and even give their lives that flying might become possible.

In 1678, Besnier, a French locksmith, constructed a curious flying machine consisting of two wooden bars which rested on his shoulders. At the ends of the bars he attached muslin wings, arranged to open on the down stroke and close on the up stroke. The wings were operated by moving the arms and legs. Although Besnier failed to realize that no man had sufficient muscular strength to fly as the bird flies, he did sense part of the truth—that gliding with the air currents was possible. During his experiments he is said to have jumped from a window sill, glided over the roof of a near-by cottage, and landed on a barge in the river.

In 1799 an Englishman, George Cayley, conceived the idea that a kite could be built large enough to carry him up into the air. Instead of a string to hold the kite against the wind he decided to use the weight of his own body. He built a huge kite with a sustaining surface of three hundred square feet. When he held on to it and ran against the wind, the kite did indeed lift and carry him some distance through the air. Cayley's kite was the first glider and also the very beginning of the modern airplane.

Wonderful though it may have seemed to him, no one paid any attention to Cayley's discovery until 1867, when F. H. Wenham, also an Englishman, came to the conclusion that if a glider were attached to a propeller driven by an engine, it would fly. Wenham was right, of course, but he left his fine logic for other men to use. He did, however, leave something else by which we may remember him. He coined the word *aëroplane*. He took the Greek *aëro*, meaning air, and joined to it the Latin *planus*, meaning flat. The British still use the world *aëroplane*, but we in America use the simpler form *airplane*.

The first successful attempt to fly was made in France on June 5, 1783, when the Montgolfier brothers demonstrated their hot-air balloon. It rose to the height of one thousand feet and remained aloft for ten minutes. Benjamin Franklin, then in France, witnessed a flight of the Montgolfier balloon and referred to it in his chronicles. (As this book tells the story of the airplane, we shall not describe in detail the free balloon.)

In Germany, another man interested in flying was experimenting. Otto Lilienthal, in the year 1890, built for himself a queer-looking glider which resembled nothing so much as a bat with huge wings. Remember Leonardo da Vinci's idea?To his bat wings Lilienthal attached a tail-like rudder for steering. For his own support on the glider he provided a pair of struts similar to the arm rests of crutches. Lilienthal would run down a hill into the wind with his glider. When sufficient speed had been attained, the glider and Lilienthal would rise triumphantly into the air. He learned to travel fair distances and was fired with the ambition to put an engine on his glider. He did design a 2½-horsepower engine, weighing ninety pounds and mounted on a biplane. Before trying his new machine, Lilienthal decided to make a short flight in his old glider. Somehow the glider stalled, one wing dropped off, and the whole thing fell to the ground, carrying Lilienthal to his death. His powered machine was never tried. Other men, however, believed that Lilienthal had been correct in his idea of flying, and his death did not stop their experiments.

About this time in America, a young man, just out of college, built a glider patterned after a sea gull. This young man was a Californian, John J. Montgomery. He worked alone and was so timid that he tried out his glider from a near-by hill at three o'clock in the morning. He was afraid that onlookers would laugh at him if his glider failed. It did not fail. He made a flight of six hundred feet—the first of many successful flights. Montgomery solved many of the problems of flight with little or no funds or encouragement. Because he worked alone and was until recently almost unknown, few written records of his work are available.

All through the nineteenth century men continued their experiments in order to bring to a reality the dream of human flight. With each generation, they moved ever closer to the fringe of the secret but never quite grasped it.

In 1842 an Englishman, W. S. Henson, was optimistic enough to patent his monoplane *Ariel* for a flight from Britain to India. Though his design had a cambered, or slightly curved, wing, tricycle landing gear, and excellent bracing, it never got beyond the model stage. Another Englishman, John Stringfellow, worked for four years on his steam-driven monoplane. It also did not progress beyond a few model flights. In 1876, a young Frenchman, Alphonse Penaud, read an article that ridiculed man's presumptuous attempts to fly. This angered the boy and he determined forthwith to conquer the air. Though lack of money balked his ambition, he constructed a number of models which contained many features found in present-day airplanes. Incidentally, Penaud was the first to use an elastic band to propel his model, as boys do. Laurence Hargrave, an American, was the first man to make a study of the cellular or box-kite type of wing construction. He confined his efforts to building models. His ideas influenced the work of Lilienthal, who incorporated them in the powered airplane he was building at the time of his death.

♦ ♦ ♦

2

AVIATION IN AMERICA IN ITS EARLY DAYS

The story of the heavier-than-air machines that flew really begins in the United States in the early 1890's. Octave Chanute, born in France and reared in America, was one of the first men to make a scientific approach to the problem of flying machines. A thorough scientist, he had followed the progress of all flight experiments the world over. He built gliders with one, two, and even five pairs of wings and tested all of them on the sand dunes of Lake Michigan. His most successful glides were made with a biplane glider. In 1894, he published a book called *Progress of Flying Machines*, which covered all the efforts of men like himself who had experimented with man-carrying gliders and flying machines. This book, without doubt, was responsible for bringing to this country the honor of being the birthplace of the first successful, man-carrying, power-driven, flying machine. A copy of Octave Chanute's book fell into the hands of two ambitious and enterprising young bicycle makers of Dayton, Ohio—Orville and Wilbur Wright.

At the time when Octave Chanute was experimenting with his gliders on the Michigan sand dunes, another aviation pioneer was hard at work in his laboratory in Washington, D. C. This man was Professor Samuel Pierpont Langley, secretary of the Smithsonian Institution. In this position he had the opportunity to pursue his studies in the aëronautical side of physics.

After much study and experimentation, he succeeded in building a tiny, steam-powered model which flew for six seconds. Langley was so much encouraged by the performance of his first model that he built a larger one. This model, weighing 26 pounds and powered with a one-horsepower steam engine, made a flight of three thousand feet in 1896.

After this flight Professor Langley felt that he had proved his theory of flight. The public became interested and the government appropriated $50,000 for Langley's use in the construction of a full-size airplane.

Langley built his plane without much difficulty, but could not find anyone to make an engine large enough for it. Finally, Charles Manley, an expert engineer, asked for permission to build the engine. Manley's engine was a five-cylinder, radial gasoline engine that developed 51 horsepower and was far ahead of its time. It was years before American radial engines were used successfully in airplanes.

Professor Langley called his machine the *Aerodrome*, and by October, 1903, the plane was ready for its test flight, with Manley to guide it. The *Aerodrome* was to be launched from a catapulting platform built on the roof of a houseboat. The houseboat was anchored on the Potomac River near Washington. As it left the platform the machine crashed into the river, and the trial was a dismal failure. The newspapers and the public ridiculed Langley, but he and Manley, who was unhurt in the crash, repaired the machine for another trial. This test took place on December 8, 1903, and again the *Aerodrome* crashed into the river. Manley once more escaped injury, but Langley and the government were abused by the public for wasting money. Langley was out of money himself, the government could not furnish funds for further trials, so the experiments were ended. The professor, discouraged and brokenhearted, gave up.

THE DREAM FULFILLED

Out in Dayton, Ohio, there were two small brothers, who dreamed, as countless other children before them had dreamed, of flying like birds through the air. Their dreams were heightened by a small toy given to them by their father, the pastor of a local church. This toy was to lead to an idea which had a profound effect on the world. You would probably call it a flying propeller. It consisted of a wooden propeller which slipped over a notched stick. By placing a finger against the propeller and rapidly pushing it up the notched stick, the propeller was made to whirl up off the end of the stick and fly into the air. The brothers, young as they were, never quite forgot this little toy as they continued to dream of flying like birds through the air.

Though the brothers continued to dream of flying, they were not the kind of lads who spent all their time in dreaming. They made kites which flew a little better and a little higher than those made by the other boys in the neighborhood. They built a press to print their own little newspaper, and they dabbled in woodcuts. To carve out porch posts for their father's home they built an eight-foot wood-turning lathe. Indeed, they were the sort of boys who caused the neighbors to say, "What will they think of next?"

Small town pastors in the early 1890's did not receive princely salaries. The brothers knew that if they ever wanted to see their dreams come true they must earn their own capital. In the early nineties America was in the midst of the bicycle craze. Everyone who could possibly afford to do so owned a bicycle of some sort and belonged to a cycle club. Being mechanically minded, the brothers did the logical thing. They set themselves up in a small bicycle shop in Dayton, next door to their home.

The bicycle shop in Dayton prospered, for the brothers were careful and expert mechanics, and cyclists in need of repairs made their way to the Wright Brothers' shop.

The two boys who had never forgotten the little toy helicopter which their father had given them years before, were Orville and Wilbur Wright. Although their bicycle shop prospered the brothers continued to dream of flying. Unlike others, who, all over the world, had been dreaming of the same thing, the dreams of the Wright Brothers persisted. They read everything that had been written about experiments in flying. Every spare moment of their time was spent in thinking about flight.

Soon after Octave Chanute's book *Progress of Flying Machines* was published in 1894, Orville and Wilbur Wright read a copy. Although they had long discussed the idea of flight, it was not until they read Chanute's book that they were able to consider seriously any experiments of their own.

Chanute's book did not give the answers to the questions in the minds of the Wright Brothers. It was primarily a record of man's attempts to fly and of his failures. However, it served its purpose because it created many more questions in the minds of Orville and Wilbur Wright. They wrote to Chanute for further information on what man had to do in order to fly.

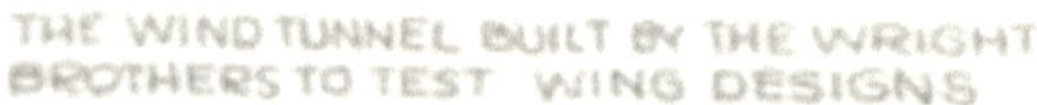
THE WIND TUNNEL BUILT BY THE WRIGHT BROTHERS TO TEST WING DESIGNS

The noted scientist answered the questions of the Wright Brothers as best he could and sent them a set of tables derived from his studies of air pressure in relation to wing surfaces. The Wrights saw in these figures a possible clue to the mysteries of flight, and in 1900 they built an experimental glider based on the information they had received from Chanute. What followed this first glider experiment is the key to the problem of why the Wright Brothers eventually succeeded while other men failed. When the glider they constructed on the principle of the then most perfect data failed to fly, they were capable of realizing that the scientific research—and not their own efforts—had been at fault.

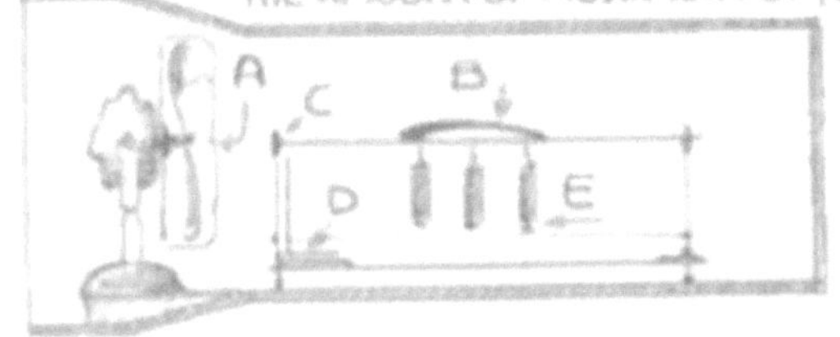

The Wright Brothers were not only inspired mechanics (as many people still believe today) but serious scientists, working along the soundest lines. In their keen desire to know what air pressure on wings really was, they cleared a corner of their bicycle shop and built a small wind tunnel with spare lumber and an old electric fan. They built small wing sections of various shapes and experimented with them in their wind tunnel. The electric fan was used to create the moving air around the wing section. By attaching the wing sections to a supporting frame and connecting the frame with a pointer and dial, they were able to keep a record of the effect of moving air on each experimental wing section. Through their wind tunnel research the Wright Brothers discovered the four forces that control all heavier-than-air flight: *lift*, *thrust*, *weight*, and *drag*. They found that a slight curve or camber in the wing section would cause the moving air to travel farther over the top of the wing surface than along the under side. This made the air pressure greater under the wing, gave a suction effect above the wing, and caused it to rise, creating *lift*. They discovered that a wing section of the proper camber would counteract the *weight* of gravity. Thus, a wing must be so designed that, with a certain amount of air flowing around it, it would lift a certain *weight*. They also discovered that air flow against any surface attached to the wing would cause a resistance or *drag*. Hundreds of experiments in their wind tunnel with various types of wing shapes gave the Wrights a series of tables from which to design a wing that would create the *lift* for a designed weight.

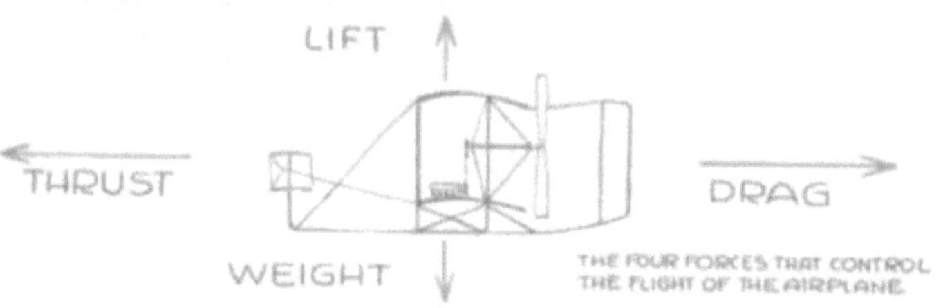

Then, after testing more than 200 wing designs and plane surfaces in their wind tunnel, the Wright Brothers found out how to figure correctly the amount of curve, or camber, that was essential to weight-carrying wings. They discovered, too, that before man could be flown through the air, he must have his wings attached firmly to a body or platform which was firm and controllable. The Wrights in their earliest experiments had realized that to be practical their machine must be built not only to fly in a straight line, but also in order that it could be steered to the right or to the left. One day, Orville was twisting a cardboard box in his hand when Wilbur noticed it. Immediately he saw the solution to the problem of steering their airplane. The result was a design which changed the *lift* of either end of the wing by warping its surface. If one end of the wing was warped to give it more *lift*, the machine would *lift* on that side and fall off into a turn. Thus the problem of steering was solved by the Wrights.

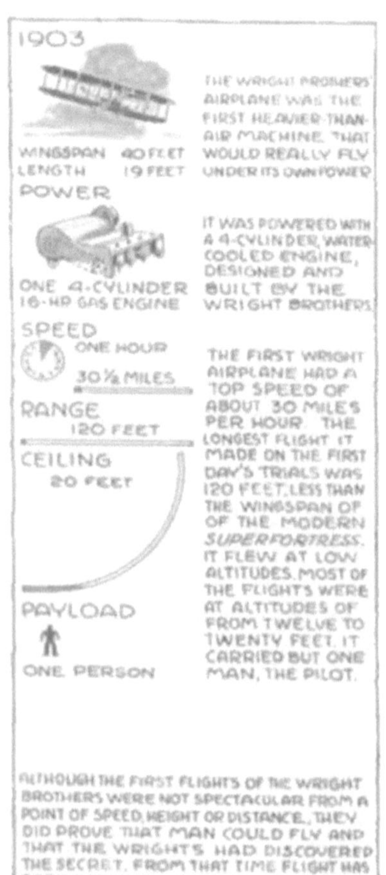

FIRST FLIGHT

After a year of exhaustive study and experiments with models in their wind tunnel, the Wright Brothers were ready to experiment with a man-carrying glider. With the thoroughness that was typical of every move of the Wrights, the brothers asked the government to let them have information on meteorological conditions all over the country. By studying the weather charts they were able to find a locality where there was a continual flow of wind. This would be nature's wind tunnel where they could test their glider day after day. Through their study of the charts they found that the wind conditions at Kitty Hawk, on the North Carolina coast, seemed to offer the best possibilities for their glider test.

Orville and Wilbur Wright began their experiments with a small man-carrying glider at Kitty Hawk in 1900. From that time until 1903 they made hundreds of successful glider flights and kept accurate records of each flight. They recorded wind velocity, angle of flight, duration of flight, time of day, temperature, humidity, and sky conditions overhead with the typical Wright attention to detail. Each year the Wrights constructed new gliders which embodied principles they had discovered for themselves during their flights at Kitty Hawk. Each glider was larger and had longer and narrower wings than the one before. During the fall of 1902 the brothers recorded nearly a thousand flights in a glider with a wingspan of thirty-two feet. It had a front elevator and a vertical tail which helped to maintain lateral stability.

By 1903 the Wright Brothers were ready to build a powered man-carrying flying machine. Their experiments had shown them just how much moving air was necessary to create lift in such a machine. To create the needed thrust, an engine having eight horsepower and weighing not over 200 pounds had to be fitted into the machine. Such an engine was not available, so the Wrights built one in their shop at Dayton, Ohio. They were ready to ship their airplane to Kitty Hawk, N. C., in the fall of 1903.

A cold wind whipped across those buff stretches of Kitty Hawk on Thursday, December 17. A coin was tossed into the air between Orville and Wilbur Wright. Orville won the toss, climbed up and stretched prone on the wing of the flying machine. He clutched the controls.

There were no cheering crowds; a mere handful of people were there. Running along its launching track, the 750 pounds of plane, engine, and passenger shot up into the air so fast that Wilbur, at the wing-tip, could not keep up. For three and one-half seconds the plane was in the air. It came to rest 105 feet from the take-off. Powered flight was born!

WRIGHT BROTHERS' AIRPLANE

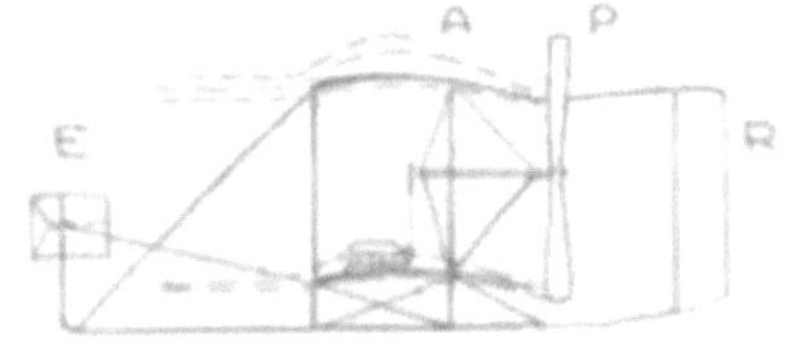

THE CURVED WING FORCES THE MOVING AIR AWAY FROM ITS UPPER SURFACE.

THIS CREATES LIGHT AIR ABOVE THE WING. THE AIR FLOWING UNDER THE WING IS NOT DISTURBED AS A RESULT IT IS HEAVIER THAN THE AIR ABOVE THE WING. THE HEAVIER AIR PUSHES THE WING UPWARD, CREATING *LIFT*.

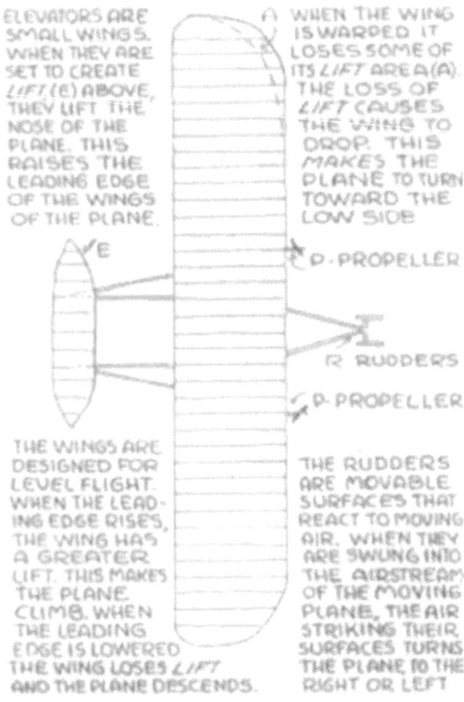

Three more flights were made on that epochal day at Kitty Hawk. The last flight of the day, with Wilbur at the controls, proved to be a breath-taking adventure. For fifty-nine seconds the roaring, white-winged craft pitched and rolled in the fitful wind. Flying low with its pilot tense at the controls, it covered a distance of 852 feet. There was no question now in the minds of Orville and Wilbur. They had proved conclusively their theory and were anxious to get back to their shop to continue improving their first flying machine.

Except for the handful of spectators who were present, the world treated the first powered flight coldly. Only a few days before the first flight of the Wright Brothers the highly publicized Langley *Aerodrome* had crashed into the Potomac for the second time. People just would not believe that the Wrights actually had flown. The newspapers refused even to print the story. Had not most newspaper editors just proved conclusively from Langley's disaster that the heavier-than-air flying machine could never work? Most scientists agreed with the newspaper editors, and the Wright Brothers were ignored by both press and public.

Immediately after their initial flight, the Wrights offered their invention to the government. The criticism aroused by the government's investment of $50,000 in the disastrous Langley experiment was too fresh in the minds of the authorities, and no encouragement was given to the brothers' offer. The Wrights returned to Dayton, where they housed their machine in a closed barn on the flat land a few miles east of the city. They admitted that they had flown, but they were among the first to state that they had only uncovered the barest physical facts associated with flight.

The brothers continued to make flights over the flat lands. They made 105 flights during the year 1904 and gained a considerable amount of experience and skill. They mastered the art of flying in a complete circle and landing the plane in the same field from which it had taken off.

Early in the winter of 1905 the Wrights began work on a new machine, incorporating many improvements resulting from their flying experience. They continued to work quietly, and the only news of them that reached the world came from the reports of farmers who lived near the flat-land flying field. Confirmed reports showed that the Wrights had now covered a distance of twenty-four miles in thirty-eight minutes.

THE FIRST AIRPLANE

Many people speak of the Wright Brothers' first airplane as a flimsy contraption of sticks, cloth, and wire. Although it was indeed built of wood, cloth and wire, it was, like everything else the Wrights built, thoughtfully and painstakingly constructed. Its wings were efficient lifting surfaces and the entire airplane was sound structurally. The main force that went into it was the result of years of sound research in aëronautical science. Orville and Wilbur Wright had solved all the fundamental problems of flight before they built their first powered, man-carrying airplane. They discovered the basic forces that control all heavier-than-air flight: *lift*, *thrust*, *drag*, and *weight*. Today, little more than forty years after the first flight at Kitty Hawk, those *four forces* discovered by the Wright Brothers still control the design of every airplane built.

Equally important was their solution of the problem of controlled flight. Their knowledge of the effect of air on the surfaces of the wings helped the Wrights solve the problem of control. By warping the wings they were able to turn the plane to the right or to the left. When a wing-tip was warped downward it increased the lift of the wing, causing it to rise. The opposite wing-tip warped upward lost lift and the plane would fall off toward the low side. The effect was that of dragging one oar of a boat in the water. To aid in turning the plane, the machine was provided with a vertical rudder attached to the lateral control. When the wings were warped, the rudder automatically swung to enforce the turn.

The pilot's right hand was on the lever which controlled the wing warping and rudder. His left was on the lever which raised and lowered the elevators. The lever at the extreme left also was attached to the elevators, providing dual control. All movements of the controls were in the direction of the desired attitude of the plane.

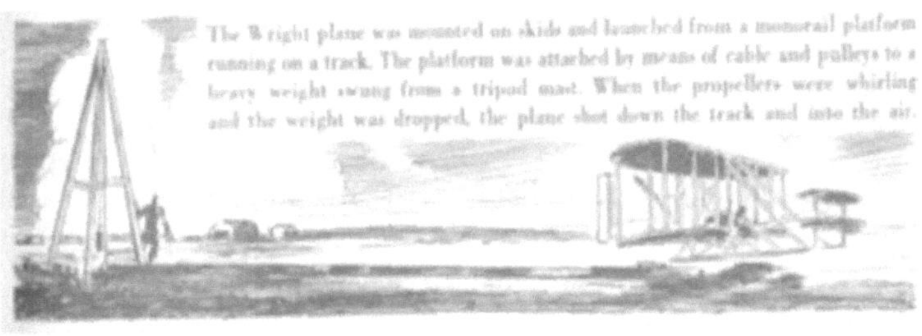

The Wright plane was mounted on skids and launched from a monorail platform running on a track. The platform was attached by means of cable and pulleys to a heavy weight swung from a tripod mast. When the propellers were whirling and the weight was dropped, the plane shot down the track and into the air.

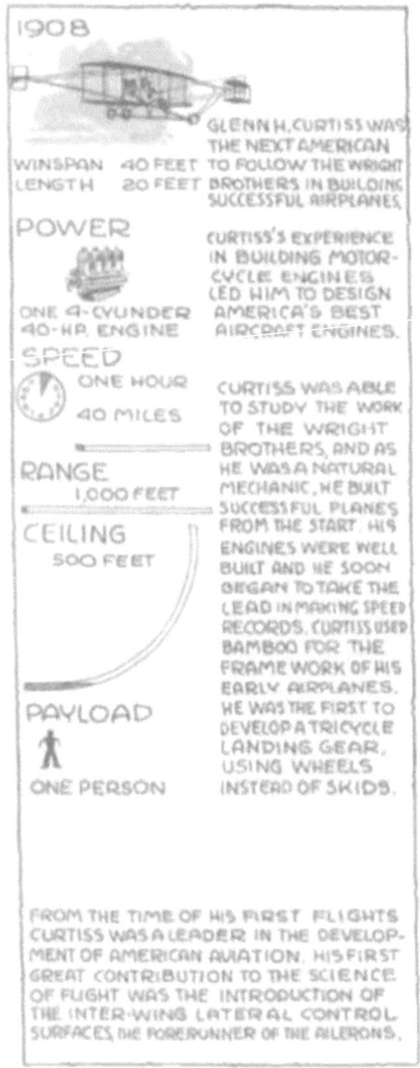

The story of American aviation began in a bicycle shop in Dayton, Ohio. It continued in the shop of a daredevil motorcycle racer and gasoline engine builder at Hammondsport, New York.

While the Wright Brothers were quietly flying their plane on the flat lands in Ohio, another self-taught, young Yankee was combining bicycles and gasoline engines to create speedy motorcycles. Speed fascinated this young man. He had started to build motorcycle engines of his own design in order to win races and break speed records.

It was not long before the name of this young mechanic began to appear repeatedly in connection with new motorcycle speed records. His name was Glenn H. Curtiss, and he won race after race. His prize money was not spent foolishly, but put into his experiments with gasoline engines.

In 1904, the pioneer American dirigible balloon builder, Captain Tom Baldwin, saw a Curtiss motorcycle in California. One look at the engine sent him scurrying to Hammondsport, New York, where he begged Glenn Curtiss to build him an engine for a new dirigible he was building. Curtiss built the engine, the first Curtiss engine to function in the skies. He also flew Tom Baldwin's dirigible, but he was not enthusiastic over the idea of flying. "Not bad sport," he remarked the first time he flew the dirigible, "but there's no place to go." Curtiss had heard of the flights of the Wright Brothers, but he was skeptical.

Before long Glenn Curtiss had another visitor. Dr. Alexander Graham Bell, the inventor of the telephone, had long been interested in the problems of flight, and had organized the Aërial Experiments Association to encourage aëronautical efforts in this country. After talking for hours, Dr. Bell converted Curtiss to a belief in the future of flying and persuaded him to join the experimental group.

In November, 1907, Glenn H. Curtiss, in company with two young Canadian engineers, F. W. Baldwin and J. A. D. McCurdy of Dr. Bell's group, and an official Army observer, Lieutenant Tom Selfridge, started to work on a new airplane. Using all of the available existing flight research and the ingenuity of Glenn H. Curtiss, the group finished their first plane in March, 1908. On March 12 Baldwin flew it 300 feet. Curtiss then designed an improved plane, the *June Bug*. With it he won the *Scientific American* contest by flying over a measured kilometer course on July 4.

AMERICA'S SECOND PLANE

In 1909, Glenn H. Curtiss, in a plane of his own design, again won the *Scientific American* award, by flying 24.7 miles over a closed course. The plane he flew was built on order for the New York Aëronautical Society. This was the first airplane order ever received by an American aircraft manufacturer.

On July 25, 1909, a Frenchman, Louis Bleriot, flew his monoplane twenty-five miles to cross the English Channel. Immediately there was furor in Europe and golden prizes were posted for new airplane developments and designs. The first big air race, the James Gordon Bennett Cup race, was held at Rheims, France, in 1909. Glenn Curtiss flew his machine against the pick of foreign pilots including Bleriot, whom he beat by six seconds to win the Cup. His speed was forty-six miles an hour.

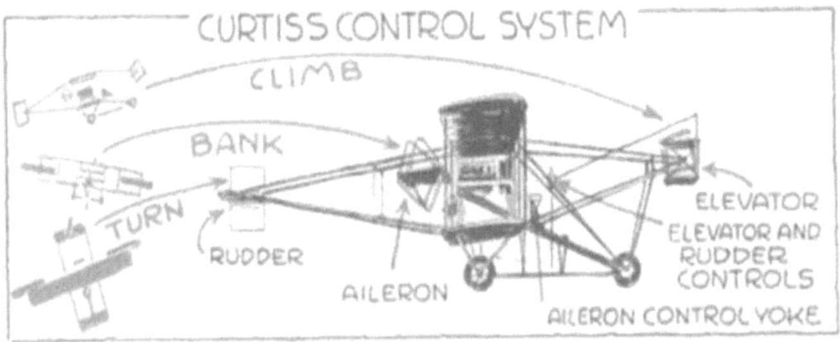

Glenn Curtiss had the benefit of the aëronautical research of the Wright Brothers to aid him in designing his first airplanes, but he could not use the wing warping method of control invented by them. This was thoroughly protected by patents. As a result, Curtiss was forced to work out a new system of lateral controls. He developed the aileron method of control for use in turns or circular flight. He did this by mounting small winglike planes on the rear struts of the plane, between the upper and lower wings. These ailerons were hinged to swing up or down and were attached by cables to a yoke which encircled the pilot's shoulders. The banking of the plane was produced by the movement of the flier as he leaned against the yoke, pushing it in the direction of the desired bank. Vertical motion was achieved by a fore and aft pressure on the control column by the flier. The wheel on the control column was attached to the vertical rudder by cables. Right or left steering was produced by turning the wheel in the desired direction. To make a climbing turn to the right, the flier would lean against the yoke, pushing to the right. At the same time he would turn his wheel gently to the right and pull the control slightly toward himself. Curtiss' method of control led the way to the modern type of wing aileron and the general system of control was basically the same as that in use today.

POWER FOR THE AIRPLANE

Going back to the four forces that govern the flight of a plane, we find *thrust* pulling the plane forward. *Thrust* is the force that keeps the plane in the air; without it the airplane could not leave the ground for sustained flight. *Thrust* is created by the propeller. The propeller blades function in the same manner as the wings. Just as the wing of a plane bites into the air to cause *lift*, the propeller blades, patterned after wing camber, bite into the air to create *thrust.* Their action on the air is similar to a screw biting its way into wood.

The propeller is whirled by the engine. Without the engine to whirl it the propeller is useless, for without *thrust* we would have no *lift.* That makes the engine the governing factor in flight. *Weight* also is a serious force in flight, and the Wrights and Curtiss found from the beginning that the four-cycle gasoline engine would give greater power for its weight than would a steam or electric engine.

The principle of the airplane engine is the same as the one used in the automobile engine. However, weight always has been a problem to aircraft designers. The automobile engine always has been too heavy for use in a plane. When the Wrights built their first plane, automobile engines weighed 25 to 35 pounds per horsepower. The Wrights built one that weighed 13 pounds per horsepower and produced 12 horsepower. They used this engine in 1903 to power their first plane. Since that time all practical airplanes have been powered with gasoline engines, designed specifically for use in heavier-than-air machines. Since the first flight, engineers constantly have strived to produce engines with greater power and less weight per horsepower. How well they have succeeded is proved by the progress of the airplane.

HOW THE FOUR-CYCLE ENGINE WORKS

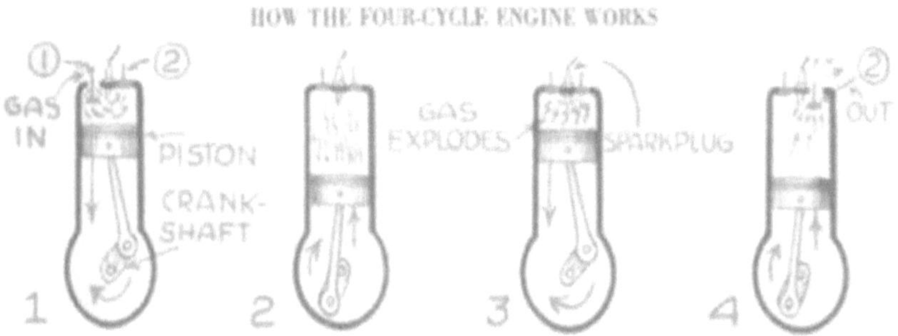

FOUR MOVEMENTS PRODUCE THE ENGINE'S POWER STROKE

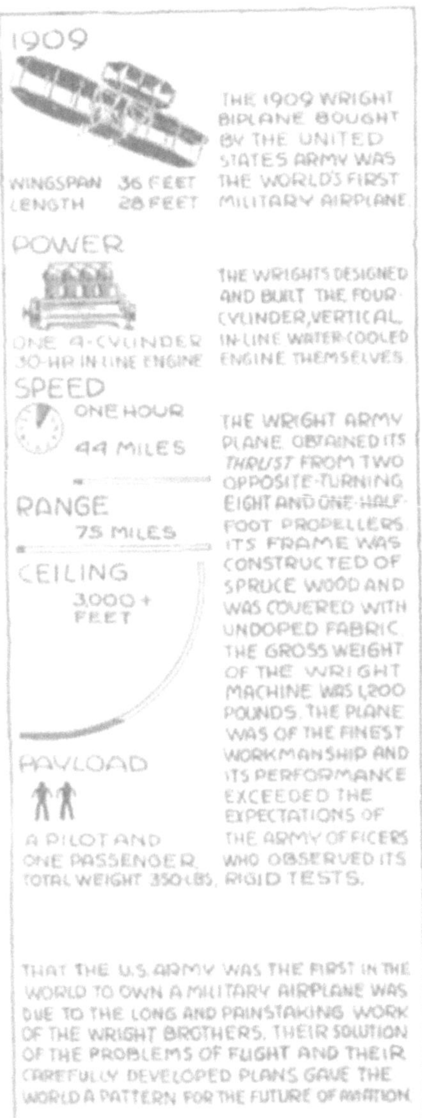

It was in 1905 that the Wright Brothers had first offered to the Army a license to use their patents; but nothing came of it. Reports coming from Dayton during the next two years, concerning their flying activities, caused the newspapers to publish a number of articles about them.

Theodore Roosevelt, then our President, was a diligent reader, and several articles about the Wrights attracted his attention. One day he clipped one of these articles from a newspaper and scribbled across it one word: "Investigate!" He passed it along to his Secretary of War, William Howard Taft. In a short time the almost forgotten Wright Brothers had a call from Brigadier General James Allen, U. S. Army Signal Corps. In the autumn of 1907 Wilbur Wright appeared in Washington to confer with the War Department.

A few months later, in July, 1907, an aëronautical division was established in the Office of the Chief Signal Officer of the Army. In December of that year the Army asked for bids on the construction of an airplane. The specifications called for a machine that could carry a weight of 350 pounds. It had to be able to remain in the air continuously for one hour with two passengers. During the flight the machine was required to remain under perfect control and to be capable of being steered in all directions. Its speed should be 40 miles per hour. The machine had to be built so that it could be taken apart and packed for transportation in army wagons. Then it had to be reassembled and put in flying condition in one hour.

By this time inventors everywhere were working on flying machines, but the Wright Brothers were the only ones who put in an appearance with an airplane for the Army trials in September, 1908.

Unfortunately the trial was a failure. The huge crowd gathered at Fort Meyer, Virginia, was horrified to see a propeller fly off and the machine crash, killing Lieutenant Tom Selfridge, the Army observer, and injuring Orville Wright. Tom Selfridge thus became the first American air martyr, and the future dimmed for the Wright Brothers and the airplane.

FIRST ARMY AIRPLANE

Fortunately, the Army considered the crash a result of material failure rather than a basic fault of the airplane. A year later, in July, 1909, Army trials again were held at Fort Meyer, with only the Wrights appearing on the scene. On July 30, Orville Wright, accompanied by Lieutenant (now Brigadier-General, retired) Frank Lahm, as the Army's observer, flew around the course, and fulfilled with ease the Army's speed and endurance specifications. The Army had its first plane, and on August 2 formal acceptance was made—just six years after man had first flown in a heavier-than-air machine. Thus the U. S. Army was the first in the world to own a military airplane.

♦ ♦ ♦

3

AMERICA BECOMES AIR-MINDED

The United States Navy also had been giving an occasional glance toward the airplane. It had been represented at the Army trials by Lieutenant G. C. Sweet and Naval Constructor William McIntee. These observers were enthusiastic and reported: "The Navy must have airplanes."

Another interested spectator was a young midshipman who had robbed his savings bank in order to witness the Army airplane trials. The young man was Donald Douglas. He, too, was most enthusiastic, but he left the trials with a vision, not of Army planes, but of giant passenger planes flying all over the world. We will hear more of him later.

On the day after the Army trials at Fort Meyer another young man far away in California headed his homemade airplane into the wind and took off on his first flight. This young fellow was Glenn L. Martin who, with the help and encouragement of his mother, had built a plane in an abandoned church in Santa Ana, California. He not only designed and built his airplane but, in addition, taught himself to fly. We will also hear more of Glenn.

As the summer of 1910 rolled around, the flights of F. W. Baldwin and Glenn Curtiss, as well as the recognition accorded the Wrights by the Army, kindled at last the public imagination. All over the country people started clamoring for a chance to see an airplane in action. As a result the Wrights and Curtiss were swamped by requests from daring young men who wanted to fly. People even wanted to buy airplanes for sport.

For the first time in its history, America had become air-minded.

The conservative Wright Brothers at last realized that the only way in which the public could be taught to understand the possibilities of the airplane was through seeing it perform. They picked a group of intelligent young daredevils and formed a flying team. This Wright flying team and a similar group under the banner of Glenn Curtiss toured the county fairs and brought aviation to the American public. In California, the twenty-year-old Glenn Martin was giving flying exhibitions to earn money with which to build bigger and better airplanes. Truly 1910 was a great year for aviation.

On May 29, 1910, Glenn Curtiss won the *New York World* prize of $10,000 for the first flight from Albany to New York City. He flew 137 miles at a speed of 54.8 miles per hour. In August another chapter in aërial history was written by the sending of a wireless message to the ground from an airplane in flight.

In September, 1910, 20,000 Bostonians had their first sight of the airplane in action when the Harvard Aëronautical Society sponsored a great aviation exhibition at Squantum, Massachusetts. The prizes, amounting to $100,000, attracted the largest group of pilots and planes ever to assemble in the United States. Claude Graham-White, the Englishman, flew a French Farman biplane and a speedy Bleriot monoplane. Another Englishman, A. V. Roe, who today builds the Avro-Lancaster, exhibited his big triplane, and the spectators were thrilled as the daring Wright and Curtiss pilots demonstrated America's best planes.

The Boston air meet was followed by an equally successful one at Belmont Park, N. Y., in October, 1910. Here daring pilots flew their planes in rain and wind, and tried many new stunts.

Ralph Johnstone, a daring Wright pilot, thrilled the crowds when he turned his plane sidewise to an almost vertical angle and then descended in a tight spiral. Walter Brookins, another Wright flier, performed his famous "short turn" in which he stood his plane vertically in the air and revolved about one wing as on a pivot. Though these pilots constantly endeavored to create new thrills for the crowds, they unconsciously were testing the capabilities of their airplanes. They also were creating the technique of flying. These early meets were the testing laboratories of aviation.

The meetings at Boston and Belmont Park served another purpose in addition to thrilling the crowds and testing the airplanes. They paved the way for the beginning of United States naval aviation. Lieutenant Charles A. Blakely, U.S.N., was ordered by the Navy Department to attend the Boston meet as an official observer. He not only observed, but he flew with Charles Willard in a Curtiss airplane. His report on the possibilities of the airplane was so enthusiastic that the Navy ordered Captain Washington Irving Chambers to keep the Navy Department informed concerning the progress of aviation in relation to its use in naval tactics.

Many of the older naval officers of that period were aligned against the airplane. They could not visualize a land airplane being used in connection with a sea-going Navy. Captain Chambers was interested in engineering and, furthermore, he was somewhat of a dreamer. But his dreams were practical. He came away from the Belmont Park air meet with the firm conviction that the airplane was satisfactory once it was in the air, and that it could be of great value to the Navy for scouting, gunfire observation, and bombing. However, to be of any great value, the airplanes must go to sea with the fleet. The airplane would offer the captain of a ship or the admiral of the fleet a magic power capable of revealing to them what lay beyond the horizon. This was Captain Chambers' dream. The Navy was fortunate in having such a farseeing officer.

As there was available at that time no airplane capable of operating from the water, the Navy was forced to adopt the idea of using a landplane. There had been considerable talk in 1910 of flying a landplane off the deck of an ocean liner for the purpose of speeding transoceanic mail delivery. In fact, arrangements were then being completed for such a test from a Hamburg-American ocean liner in New York. But Captain Chambers was not a man to allow the United States Navy to come in second in such an experiment. If an airplane could be flown from the deck of a vessel, let it be a Navy ship. The cruiser U. S. S. *Birmingham* was placed at the Captain's disposal and he went to work immediately preparing for the first attempt to fly an airplane from the deck of a ship. He had a temporary platform erected on the fore deck of the *Birmingham*. It was built of planks, was eighty-three feet long and twenty-eight feet wide, and sloped downward toward the bow of the ship.

As the Navy had no pilots, a civilian flier, Eugene Ely, was lent for the test by Glenn Curtiss, whose plane was being used. On Monday, November 14, 1910, in the most unfavorable weather, Ely rolled across the platform into the rain and mist. At the end of the platform his plane dived toward the water. Ely pulled up on his elevators and flew on. He landed on a sand bar after a flight of two and one-half miles, and another chapter in naval history was made.

♦ ♦ ♦

4

THE ARMY AND NAVY SPREAD THEIR WINGS

Although successful, Eugene Ely's flight from the deck of the *Birmingham* had little effect on the Navy's conservative attitude toward aviation. At times, as the skeptical comments of naval officers continued, it appeared that Captain Chambers was being dared to prove the value of the airplane to the Navy. It was fortunate for the United States that the Captain was an officer willing to accept the challenge.

Captain Chambers asked for funds to purchase several of the existing types of airplanes for the purpose of training navy personnel in the art of flying. As no money was available, the Captain had to continue his experiments in co-operation with aircraft manufacturers and civilian fliers. Spurred by the successful flight of Ely, Glenn Curtiss willingly aided Captain Chambers. Curtiss was so enthusiastic about the future of naval aviation that he approached the Navy Department with the offer to train, without cost to the service, an officer to fly. After considerable discussion in the Department, Lieutenant Theodore G. Ellyson, U. S. Navy, was ordered to join Curtiss.

Curtiss moved his flying activities to San Diego, California, in 1910, and it was there that Lieutenant Ellyson became the first American naval officer to learn to fly. This was eight years after the first flights of the Wright Brothers.

Curtiss had collected a group of skilled pilots to fly under his direction. In this group were McCurdy, Willard, Witmer, Ely, and the famous Lincoln Beachey. With this assemblage Curtiss was able to make great strides in the progress of flying and aircraft development. Curtiss and Captain Chambers, working closely together, laid their plans for proving to the Navy Department the capabilities of the airplane. Both men were convinced thoroughly that it was possible to take off in an airplane from the deck of a ship, fly to a designated spot, fly back, and land on the deck. There was a great amount of ridicule at this idea, but Curtiss and Chambers went ahead with their plans and erected a 120-foot platform on the deck of the cruiser U. S. S. *Pennsylvania.* On January 18, 1911, a Curtiss landplane, with Eugene Ely at the controls, soared from the deck, circled out over the water, and approached the cruiser. Twenty-two pairs of fifty-pound sandbags were attached to lines drawn taut across the deck platform. The plane was equipped with steel hooks for use in catching the deck lines. Ely flew in at the speed of thirty-nine miles an hour. Sailorsaboard the *Pennsylvania* ducked for cover, expecting the plane to overshoot the platform. Just as he reached the end of the platform, Ely pulled up the nose of his ship, and cut off the engine. The plane settled to the deck. Then and there were the beginnings of what eventually was to become the most effective weapon of the United States Navy—the *aircraft carrier.*

During the winter of 1911, Curtiss designed the first American seaplane, or hydroplane as it was then called. On January 26th, he made a flight of thirty-one seconds and landed smoothly on the water. That afternoon he made a number of flights, to the delight of the crowds that lined the Coronado shores of the Spanish Bight off San Diego. Little did the onlookers dream that years later flying boats of the United States Navy would fly over the Seven Seas, even remaining aloft for a day at a time.

In addition to Lieutenant Ellyson, Captain Chambers succeeded in having Lieutenants John H. Towers and John Rogers ordered to report for flight instruction. These three men became Navy Pilots One, Two and Three. Pilot Number 3 was Lieutenant (now Vice Admiral) John H. Towers, who ever since has made his name synonymous with the progress of naval aviation. In July, 1911, the United States Navy took delivery of its first airplanes, one Wright and two Curtiss landplanes. Later that year the Navy established its first aviation camp on the banks of Severn River just across from the Naval Academy at Annapolis, Maryland.

During this time the United States Army was making some progress with military aviation. In March, 1911, Congress was prevailed upon to appropriate $125,000 for aëronautics. The Army bought three more airplanes, the first since the purchase of one Wright airplane in 1909. In July, 1911, the first military aviation school was established at College Park, Maryland. The Army's first instructor was Army Pilot Number 1, Lieutenant Frank Lahm. The first students were Lieutenants Benjamin Foulois, Thomas DeW. Milling, and the man who was destined, thirty-two years later, to lead the world's greatest air force, Henry H. ("Hap") Arnold, Commanding General, United States Army Air Forces during World War II.

Flying in two Wright and one Curtiss biplanes, the fledgling Army fliers conducted experimental work in aërial photography and radio. But these forward-looking young men, even then, saw the airplane as a weapon and began seeking ways of dealing out destruction to an enemy. They fired machine guns at ground targets, tested a bomb sight, and dropped small bombs from their planes.

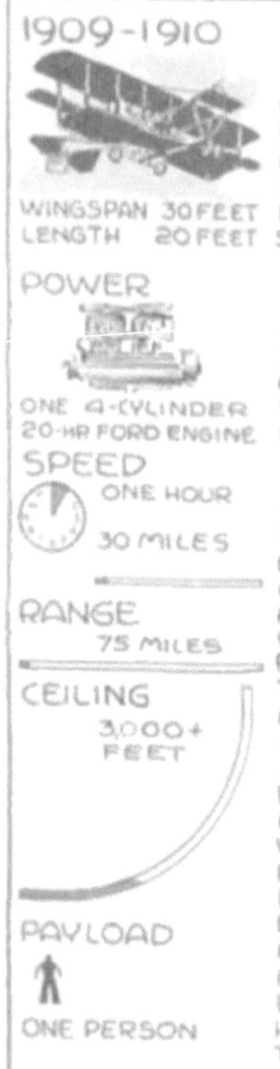

In 1905 a newspaper in Salina, Kansas, had carried a story of two brothers named Wright. This story robbed the budding "auto" industry of a promising young mechanic, Glenn L. Martin by name.

As a boy, Glenn Martin built and flew the very best kites in Salina. As he grew older he was thrilled by the appearance of the horseless carriage. As soon as he was old enough he took a job in Dave Methven's garage, convinced that there was a future in the noisy "gas-buggies."

In the surge of interest in automobiles, Glenn Martin had all but forgotten the stories of

Chanute and Lilienthal and the old urge of the winds in his kites. In 1905, after reading the newspaper story concerning the Wrights, he excitedly told his mother, "I am going to fly, too!" And he did.

A short time after he made that remark, Glenn's family moved to California and he soon became a successful automobile salesman. But he did not forget his decision to fly. With his mother's support, he began to build his plane by night, after selling cars all day. With his mother holding a lantern for him, he often worked most of the night in the abandoned church that served as his workshop. In spite of neighborly criticism, Glenn finished his plane and flew it from a Santa Ana cow pasture, on August 1, 1909.

As soon as he had successfully flown his first airplane, Martin began to plan better machines. He gave flying exhibitions all over southern California to earn the money to build more Martin planes. In January, 1912, he flew the first mail from Dominguez, California, to Compton, California. In April of that year he flew twenty-four miles in twenty-five minutes, to deliver newspapers from Fresno, California, to a neighboring town. On May 10, 1910, Martin flew thirty-three miles over the ocean from Newport Harbor, California, to Catalina Island. This first trans-Pacific flight was made in a hydroplane of Martin's own design.

♦ ♦ ♦

5

UNITED STATES MILITARY AND NAVAL AVIATION

WORLD WAR I

Although America was actually the birthplace of the airplane, many years passed after the first flight of the Wright Brothers before there was any real consideration of the military or civil values of aviation. That aviation did progress at all in its early years was due to the efforts of a few fledgling military fliers, a group of barnstormers, and a handful of aircraft builders.

Working closely together, these men flew and experimented with our first flying machines. They risked their lives time and again in order to learn everything possible about flying and the flying machine. As a result of crashes and hairbreadth escapes, these men discovered many faults and set about correcting them.

Each make of plane had a different control system, and an all-around flier had to master several varieties of levers and wheels in order to be able to fly all types of machines. A pilot originally was forced to fly his plane while sitting on an exposed and uncomfortable perch at the edge of the wing. Just back of his seat was mounted the heavy engine ready to topple over on him in case of a crash.

The first step in correcting some of the faults of the early airplane came with the development of a body, or fuselage. The first fuselages were built of spruce frames covered with fabric and strengthened with wire. They were mounted between the wings and braced to them. The engine and propeller were housed in the front of the fuselage. Farther back an enclosed compartment, or cockpit, was provided for the pilot. Thus he was moved from his perch on the wing with the engine at his back into a safer and more comfortable location.

The development of the fuselage caused the elevators to be taken away from the front of the machine. These were combined with the stabilizer and rudder attached to the rear of the fuselage. The Wright method of wing warping to produce lateral control was dispensed with and the Curtiss type of aileron was moved up from the wing struts and hinged to the trailing edge of the wings. This established the ailerons as part of the *lift* surfaces of the wings, giving them a more direct influence on the lateral movements of the airplane.

With the new positions of the control surfaces came the second important step, the standard control system. This system made use of a single control column, or stick, and a rudder bar. The stick was attached by means of cables and pulleys to both the ailerons and the elevators. A hinged arrangement allowed the stick to be moved forward and backward, and to the right or to the left. The forward and backward movement of the stick controlled the up and down position of the elevators. The right and left movement of the stick raised or lowered the ailerons. Steering to right or left was accomplished by pressure of the pilot's feet on a bar that was attached to the rudder by cables. All positions of the airplane were caused by gently pressing the control stick and rudder bar in the direction of the flight movement desired by the pilot.

By 1915, American airplane builders had adopted a standard biplane design with an enclosed fuselage and a two-wheel and tail-skid landing gear, typified by the Curtiss *Jenny* at the left.

The beginning of World War I, in Europe, saw the first use of the airplane by the military. At first, warring pilots flying over the battle lines actually exchanged friendly waves in passing. This was the expression of brotherly feeling among men who already had risked their lives to conquer the flying machine.

But this knightly feeling did not last long. One belligerent flier carried a rifle aloft. This rifle inspired the thought of the machine gun, and war in the air, as in the trenches, became a survival of the fittest.

In the United States, the Aviation Section, Signal Corps, U. S. Army, was just two weeks old. When it was created on July 18, 1914, the Aviation Section had an authorized personnel of 60 officers and 260 enlisted men, and a few airplanes. In Europe, every major power boasted of hundreds of planes.

The year 1916, two years after the start of World War I, saw Army aviation in its first offensive action. Eight low-powered planes engaged in a punitive expedition against Mexican bandits. The chief result of this expedition was the severe newspaper criticism of the poor showing made by our fliers and America's lack of improved types of combat planes.

As the result of the criticism created by the Mexican expedition, Congress, in June, 1916, voted funds for the expansion of Army aviation. But aviation development required time and, actually, when the United States went into World War I on April 6, 1917, Army aviation consisted of but 65 officers (including only 35 fliers), 1,087 enlisted men, and 55 airplanes. All of the planes were obsolete and none carried machine guns.

Thus, with no military planes suitable for use against a well-equipped enemy, no fliers trained in the use of high-powered fighting planes and aërial machine guns, and with few factories that had had any previous experience in the production of airplanes, America plunged into the midst of World War I.

Although a little late, America went to work. Having no good combat designs of our own, our fliers fought in British and French airplanes. We developed the best training plane in the world, the Curtiss JN-*Jenny* (page 32), and trained 15,000 flying cadets. By March, 1918, our Army Aviation strength was 11,000 officers and 120,000 enlisted men. At the time of the Armistice we had 757 pilots, 481 observers, with 740 planes at the front and 1,402 pilots and 769 airplanes in the Zone of Advance, ready for combat. Our pilots were credited with the destruction of 491 enemy airplanes, of which 462 were accounted for by 63 airmen. We had produced 26 aces, each of whom had destroyed five or more enemy aircraft.

♦ ♦ ♦

6

THE FIRSTTRANSATLANTICFLIGHT

United States naval aviation had made slow but steady progress in the years just preceding World War I. Bombing and scouting practice was engaged in by naval planes and considerable headway was made in the development of larger flying boats and amphibians.

When war was declared in 1917, naval aviation consisted of 54 airplanes, 38 pilots, and 163 enlisted men. By rapid expansion it had reached the strength of more than 50,000 men and over 2,000 airplanes by the end of the war. Some 17,000 men and 540 airplanes were sent abroad during the conflict. Extremely successful anti-submarine and patrol operations were carried on throughout the war, and our naval aviators served with great distinction.

Our early models of big flying boats, like the F5-L above, were so successful that the Navy ordered even larger ones. The "big boats" as they were termed, were giant four-engine planes with a wingspan of 126 feet, the largest built to that time. Their size created a difficult shipping problem and it was decided that they were to be flown overseas. Commander John H. Towers, pioneer naval operator, was assigned to the task of supervising their construction and flight tests. The planes were ordered in December, 1917, and ten months later the first of the "big boats" proved its ability in a series of test flights. The planes were designated the NC's, Navy Curtiss. With everyone rushing madly to finish the NC's for their overseas flight, the war ended abruptly.

After the Armistice the NC's were not needed in Europe, but they were ready and the Navy felt sure that they could fly the Atlantic. On May 6, 1919, three NC's took off from Far Rockaway, New York, on one of the most significant flights in history. After making a stop at Trepassey Bay, Newfoundland, the NC's with "Jack" Towers in command, flew through the stormy Atlantic night to land the following morning on the water near Horta in the Azores. The planes were badly battered, and the crews were weary. Only the NC-4 Lieutenant Commander A. C. Read in charge, flew on to Lisbon, Portugal, and finally to Plymouth, England, in the first transatlantic flight.

A month after the first transatlantic flight of the U. S. Navy NC boats, two Royal Flying Corps pilots, Captain John Alcock and Lieutenant Arthur Brown, flying a two-engined Vickers Vimy biplane, flew nonstop from Newfoundland to Ireland. To those two hardy adventurers goes the credit for the first nonstop crossing of the Atlantic by airplane.

♦ ♦ ♦

7

MEN AND MACHINES, WORLD WAR I

Slow as she had been in starting, America picked up speed and finished World War I with a record definitely creditable. American aviation discarded its swaddling clothes forever. At the time of the Armistice, American fliers had flown more than 3,500,000 miles in battle and dropped 275,000 pounds of explosives on the Germans. In plane-to-plane combat our military pilots showed a courage and initiative unequaled by ally or foe.

With our entry into the war, our infant aviation industry also picked up speed. With typical American energy it built up an enviable production record before the end of the war. As America had no combat airplane designs at the start of the war, our industry turned out planes and engines of foreign design. Aircraft factories built English DH-4 observation planes, Handley-Page bombers, and SE-5 fighter planes. We did build one plane of American design, the Curtiss JN-4 *Jenny* training plane. The *Jenny* was the best training plane in the world at that time. Our factories built hundreds of them in 1917 and 1918. Practically all American and many Allied fliers received their flight training in the famous old *Jennies*.

The science of flight was only slightly more than ten years old when men decided to use the airplane as a military weapon in actual warfare. Therefore it can be understood that the fighting planes of World War I were fairly elementary in every way. They were fairly standard in design and construction—all biplanes with enclosed fuselage and two-wheel and tail-skid landing gear. The French Nieuport-27 fighter plane, brought out in 1915, was considered the outstanding aërial achievement of its day. The first of the British fighters was the Sopwith *Camel*. The Nieuport-27 was followed in 1916 by the famous French Spad and in 1917 by the Nieuport-28. The Germans used the Fokker fighter designed by Anthony Fokker, a Hollander.

Fighter planes of World War I had an average wingspan of 28 feet, and a ceiling of about 20,000 feet. They were powered with engines of 150 horsepower, their speeds ranged from 100 to 125 miles per hour. Their average weight was 1,500 pounds and they carried enough gasoline for a two hours' flight and were armed with two .30-caliber machine guns.

All of these planes had the habit of shedding parts under stress of battle and more pilots were killed during the war because of defective equipment, lack of parachutes, and inexperience than as a result of enemy action.

The long-range heavy bomber also came into being during World War I. Before the conflict was over many farsighted military men visualized it as the most important military weapon produced by the science of flight. Our own General "Billy" Mitchell was one of the first to visualize its possibilities.

The British two-engined Handley-Page bomber carried the brunt of heavy bombardment action during the war. It carried a one-thousand-poundbomb load, with its bombs ranging from 15 to 600 pounds each. It had a range of 250 miles and was credited with a great deal of destructive work behind the German lines. At the end of the war a new and larger Handley-Page bomber with a range of 650 miles and a 2-ton bomb load capacity was ready to carry the war far beyond the enemy's lines. While the Germans relied mainly on their big Zeppelins for long-range bombardment, they also used the big two-engined *Gotha* bomber for raids on French cities.

Whether the airplane had any real effect on the outcome of World War I is questionable. It did, however, set keen-minded military men to thinking in a manner that made the airplane the key weapon of World War II.

During World War I, American aviation production was centered around the three great names that had typified the airplane since its earliest days—Wright, Curtiss, and Martin. Wilbur Wright died on May 30, 1912, from typhoid fever, and in 1915 Orville disposed of his interests in the Wright Company. He continued, however, to act as a consultant for the company. In California, young Glenn L. Martin's company had prospered with war orders from the United States and foreign governments. His chief engineer was the young midshipman who, not so many years before, had robbed his penny bank to watch the trials of the first Wright Army plane—Donald Douglas. Larry Bell, of whom we will hear more in connection with another great war, was Martin's general manager. In 1916, the Martin Company and the Wright Company were joined in partnership, as the Wright-Martin Company. This organization was a heavy contributor to the war effort, turning out hundreds of airplane engines for the Allies. The Curtiss company produced the famous Jenny training plane and many flying boats for the Navy, including the big

NC flying boats. America also produced the celebrated 12-cylinder, 450-horsepower *Liberty* engine. It was the lightest per horsepower aviation engine in the World and was used to power the American-built DH-4 observation plane used by the Army in the latter part of the war. Considering the fact that it was only a dozen years since man had first flown in a powered airplane and that our knowledge of aërial warfare was extremely limited, both manufacturers and aviators did a splendid job in the First World War.

It was in terms of men rather than in aërial victories that America profited. As the result of the foundation laid by men like Wilbur and Orville Wright, Glenn H. Curtiss, Glenn L. Martin, E. J. Hall and J. G. Vincent (inventors of the Liberty engine), Guy Vaughn of Curtiss, Donald Douglas, and others, America gained world leadership in the production of aircraft engines and airplanes.

Many of the young men who flew the "crates" of World War I for the American Army and Navy are the men whose names make headlines in commercial air transport and on the world-wide battlefronts today. Many a pilot who got his first flying training in a *Jenny* or a Curtiss flying boat is now an airline executive or a world-famous flying general or admiral. It was the steadfast efforts of such veteran airmen as Mitchell, Arnold, Spaatz, Eaker, Rickenbacker, Harold L. George, Artemus Gates, Bob Lovett, Louis Brereton, Jimmy Doolittle, Frank Lahm, Gill Robb Wilson, Jack Jouett, John H. Towers, and others, who have built American air supremacy.

The famous Curtiss *Jenny* that served the Army so well as a training plane also helped keep aviation alive in the days following World War I. Ex-Army fliers used them for pleasure and business, and a few of them used them to start some of the country's first airlines.

♦ ♦ ♦

8

THE FIRST AIR MAIL

On May 15, 1918, America's first official airplane mail service was inaugurated. The man in charge was Major Reuben H. Fleet, U. S. Army Air Service. We will hear more of Major Fleet later on in our story.

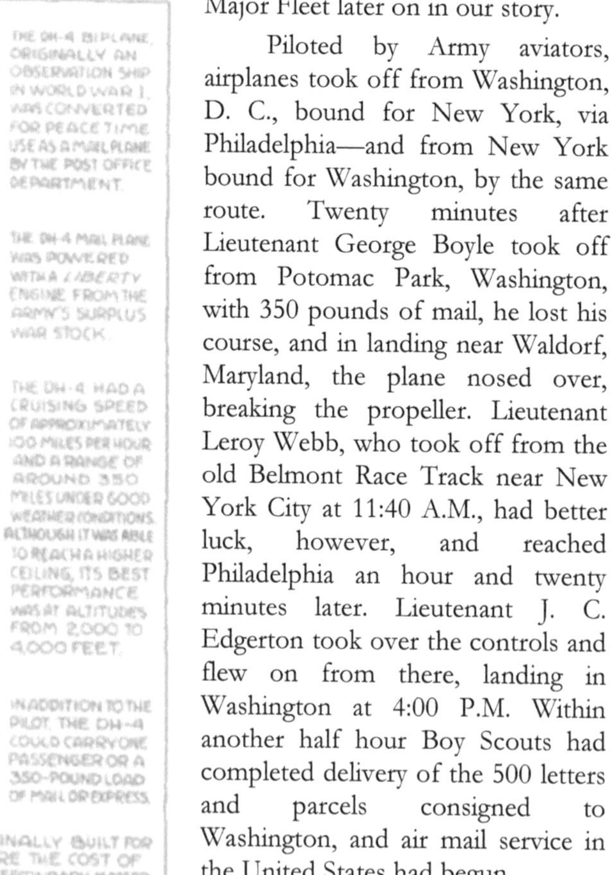
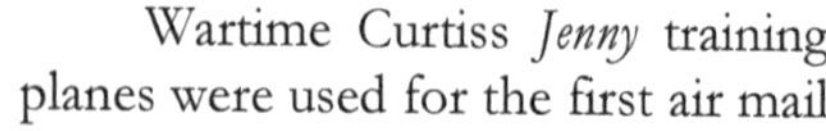

Piloted by Army aviators, airplanes took off from Washington, D. C., bound for New York, via Philadelphia—and from New York bound for Washington, by the same route. Twenty minutes after Lieutenant George Boyle took off from Potomac Park, Washington, with 350 pounds of mail, he lost his course, and in landing near Waldorf, Maryland, the plane nosed over, breaking the propeller. Lieutenant Leroy Webb, who took off from the old Belmont Race Track near New York City at 11:40 A.M., had better luck, however, and reached Philadelphia an hour and twenty minutes later. Lieutenant J. C. Edgerton took over the controls and flew on from there, landing in Washington at 4:00 P.M. Within another half hour Boy Scouts had completed delivery of the 500 letters and parcels consigned to Washington, and air mail service in the United States had begun.

Wartime Curtiss *Jenny* training planes were used for the first air mail service. They could carry about 300 pounds of mail and had a top speed of 90 miles per hour. In August, 1918, the air mail service was taken over by the Post Office Department.

THE FIRST ATTEMPT AT PASSENGER COMFORT A TWO-PLACE CABIN INSTALLED IN A DH-4 BY AIR MAIL MECHANICS IN 1920

The original air mail route of 1918 was only 218 miles in length, but it was not long before the Post Office Department extended the service. By September, 1920, transcontinental air mail service was in operation between New York and San Francisco, California.

Flying in single-engined, open-cockpit Army *Jennies* and DH-4's, the unsung pioneers of our early air mail service were Army aviators. They had no reliable flight instruments. Roads, rivers, and railroad tracks were their only airway markers, and the family wash on a clothes line was the means by which the fliers ascertained their wind direction.

♦ ♦ ♦

9

PRECISION BOMBING IS BORN

The end of World War I found Army aviation with a personnel of 18,000 officers and 135,000 enlisted men. Aircraft manufacturers with expanded production facilities were proceeding at full speed. Within a very short time the aviation strength of the Army was reduced to 1,000 officers and 10,000 enlisted men. Aircraft contracts were canceled and soon after the close of the war many aircraft firms were forced out of business. As a result, the Army was left to carry on with reconditioned wartime airplanes and engines.

Men like General "Billy" Mitchell fought to keep the Army from forgetting aviation. This was a peace-loving country and most people felt that the United States had fought its last war. Mitchell organized a transcontinental air race. He tried to persuade the Government to build lighted airways across the country for commercial aviation, but met with little support. Ex-Army aviators bought discarded Army planes, barnstormed the country, carried passengers at five dollars a hop, and tried in every way possible to keep aviation alive. But the early twenties saw aviation in an almost hopeless struggle for existence.

The three big names of aviation continued to lead in the struggling airplane manufacturing field. The Wright-Martin Company separated. The Wright interests became the Wright Aëronautical Corporation and those of Martin became the Glenn L. Martin Company. The Wright organization made airplane engines, and the Martin Company, with Glenn L. Martin still its director, began to build a big two-engine bomber. The Curtiss Company continued to build airplanes.

The devastating raids made by our big bombers on enemy lands, led many people to believe that the heavy bomber of the Army Air Forces was a "miracle" weapon born of World War II. Airmen know better. In World War I, General Mitchell believed that heavy long-range bombers could have bombed Germany to a more decisive defeat. However, we had no heavy bombers in 1918. It was not until 1921 that General Mitchell had an opportunity to prove the destructive power of aërial bombs.

In July of that year, using six Martin BM-1 bombers, the Army sank the giant 22,000-ton, ex-German battleship *Ostfriesland* with aërial bombs in 25 minutes. "Billy" Mitchell's theory was proved and America's policy of long-range, precision bombing was born.

♦ ♦ ♦

10

THE U. S. NAVY'S FIRST AIRCRAFT CARRIER

Ever since that morning in January, 1911, when Eugene Ely took off from a platform on the deck of the cruiser *Pennsylvania*, flew around, and landed back on the deck, farsighted naval leaders had dreamed of taking the airplane to sea with the fleet.

World War I and the use of naval aviation in anti-submarine and patrol duties had stopped progress in experiments along this line. It was not until the end of the war that Navy men began to consider the idea of building a surface vessel capable of carrying airplanes to sea. It was soon recognized that such a ship must be devoted exclusively to the carrying and handling of airplanes. It must be literally an aircraft carrier.

The idea of the carrier created several problems. Assuming that the pilots could land on the bobbing deck of a vessel, how were the planes to be stopped? Then there was the question of training flying boat pilots to handle landplanes. While some Navy pilots had obtained landplane experience overseas during the war, the majority had never been aloft in any type of machine other than a seaplane.

Nevertheless, the entire idea appealed to our Navy men and the project was undertaken. The Army agreed to provide landplane training facilities for Navy pilots. Under the command of Lieutenant Commander G. DeC. Chavalier, U.S.N., the Navy pilots first mastered the technique of flying landplanes. They learned to land their planes in small areas marked out on the ground to represent the deck of a ship. Then a platform one hundred feet long and forty feet wide was constructed on a coal barge at the Washington Navy Yard for use in deck landings. The barge platform proved dangerous, since no arresting gear had yet been developed, and the training was continued at the Navy Yard in Philadelphia. Here a platform was erected on the ground and a number of arresting gear ideas were tested. Finally there was developed a simple and reliable arresting gear, an outgrowth of the original taut line and sandbag idea, used by Ely.

In the meantime, the secretary of the Navy had authorized the conversion of the old collier, *Jupiter*, into an aircraft carrier. A platform, or flight deck, was built covering the entire top of the ship and the arresting gear was mounted on it at the stern. The ship's smokestacks were set to one side of the deck so as not to interfere with the landings. The carrier, commissioned the *Langley*, in memory of the inventive professor, first steamed to sea in October, 1922. At a spot near Old Point Comfort, where eleven years before Ely had made his flight from the *Birmingham*, Commander V. C. Griffin soared up from the deck of the *Langley*.

Out from Norfolk roared Commander Chavalier, to set his plane down in a perfect landing on the *Langley's* deck. The United States Navy had its first aircraft carrier.

♦ ♦ ♦

11

THE FIRST FLIGHT AROUND THE WORLD

Do you remember the young midshipman who spent his savings to go to see the Wrights fly their plane for the Army at Fort Meyer? After that it was not long before he decided to leave the Naval Academy to take up a career in the new field of aviation. By 1920 Donald Douglas was one of America's most promising aircraft engineers. At the age of twenty-eight he was vice president of the Glenn L. Martin Company. At that age most young men would have been happy to be even close to a position like that. But not Don Douglas. He still had his dream of great commercial airliners and he thought that California was the place to build them. He left his job with Martin and started in business for himself, at a time when half the aviation industry was struggling for its very existence.

Douglas went to Los Angeles, but friends and bankers alike could see no future in aviation, and advised him to get out of it. Discouraged but not beaten, he kept on trying. A chance meeting with a wealthy man in a barber shop gave him his starting capital and before long the former midshipman was building planes for the U. S. Navy. In 1924, his Army Douglas World Cruiser circled the globe, but his great airliners still were a dream.

It was between April 6 and September 28, 1924, that the first flight around the world was made. Four Douglas Cruisers, each carrying two men, started the flight from Seattle, Washington. A world-wide organization was set up to service the planes as they circled the globe. Two of the planes completed the trip 175 days later. The total distance flown was 26,345 miles and the total flying time was 363 hours, 7 minutes. A third plane was destroyed in a crash in Alaska early in the flight, and the fourth sank after a crash in the Atlantic on the last lap of the trip. The DWC's used in the flight were powered with 450-horsepower *Liberty* engines, and the average speed was about 72 miles per hour. This round-the-world flight was truly a daring operation.

12

AIR PROGRESS

In the early twenties the design of the airplane underwent very little change. The biplane with an enclosed fuselage remained standard in both military and civil aircraft. With the exception of a few Navy flying boats, the biplane was a two-place plane capable of carrying the pilot and one passenger, or 300 pounds of cargo or mail. There were some attempts at streamlining to eliminate drag, but they consisted mainly of using fewer wing struts and wire bracings.

Landing gears were made stronger and the oleo landing strut was introduced. The oleo landing strut was made by two sleevelike cylinders which operated as does a piston. The upper cylinder was filled with heavy oil. The landing wheels were attached to the lower cylinder. On landing, the weight of the airplane caused the cylinder to push up, as a piston, into the oil-filled upper cylinder. This produced a pressure on the oil. A small opening in the cylinder allowed the oil slowly to slip out of the cylinder. This reduced the pressure gradually as the gear absorbed the landing shock. If you take a bicycle pump and hold your finger over the valve, then build up pressure in the pump and at the same time allow just a little air to escape from under your finger, you will readily see how the oleo landing works. The oleo shock-absorbing type of landing gear is standard with all modern planes.

Fuselage construction of wooden stringers and posts, with the wire bracing so familiar in all early airplanes, gave way to the use of veneered wood covering. The first Douglas planes, the DH-4's, the Curtiss Orioles, and the L. W. F. of the early twenties used veneer covering instead of fabric for their fuselages. This was followed by the introduction of welded steel tubing for fuselage framework. Several attempts were made to develop a monoplane in those days but none was very successful. In Germany, in 1922, the Junkers JL6 was the first plane successfully to use an internally braced monoplane wing. In this country it was several years before an aircraft designer dared to attempt to overcome the prejudiced aviators against the monoplane design.

During the middle twenties the names of Wright, Curtiss, and Martin were still to the fore. The Wright Aëronautical Corporation was the leader in its field. Its liquid-cooled engines had grown from 120-horsepower to 300-, 400-, 675-horsepower. It also had begun to experiment with and develop an air-cooled radial airplane engine. This engine, invented by Charles L. Lawrance, was a result of his study of the Manley radial engine built for Professor Langley's *Aerodrome.* The Manley engine was far ahead of its time. What might have happened had the first Wright plane and the Manley engine come together in the early days is pure guesswork. The original Manley radial engine weighed only 3.6 pounds per horsepower. In the early twenties, when Lawrance started to work with the Manley engine as a guide, airplane engines weighed about 10 pounds per horsepower. The Manley engine used in the *Aerodrome* was water-cooled and Lawrance went to work to eliminate the extra weight caused by radiator and water-cooling equipment. So successful were his first experiments that he joined the Wright Aëronautical Corporation to collaborate in developing an aircraft engine that was to have a profound influence on world aviation.

During this time the Curtiss Company continued to build successful airplanes for both the Army and the Navy, including the first of the famous Hawk fighters, completed in 1923. Martin worked on improved types of Army bombers and Douglas built planes for both branches of the service. In Seattle, Washington, the Boeing Company had started its first aircraft for the Army. New names such as Beech, Cessna, Sikorsky, Vought, Fairchild, Northrop, and others began to appear on the nameplates of new planes.

In the early twenties, with transcontinental mail service well under way, there were many attempts made to establish air transport and cargo services. Most of these ventures were undertaken by former military aviators, using cast-off Army airplanes. Their airports usually were cow pastures. They planned their own air routes and got their weather reports from the newspapers. Bad weather would often ground a flight and passengers were almost as uncertain as the weather. Many of those pioneer operators had to depend on the dollar-a-ride hops of Sunday sightseers to "keep the wolf from the door." One service operated 14-passenger converted Navy seaplanes on a route between New York and Havana, and another route between Cleveland and Detroit. Most of these pioneer air transport Operations lasted for only a short time, due to the heavy cost of maintaining the planes and the lack of properly marked air routes.

Difficulties had arisen in the air mail service by 1921. It had become apparent that air mail would not be valuable to the Government unless it could be flown by night as well as by day. It had been standard practice for the mail to be flown only during daylight hours and to be carried by train at night. The Government was about to abandon the air mail service when the pilots pointed out that all that was needed was a chain of airway beacons and lights for the landing fields and planes.

To prove their point a group of pilots volunteered to make a continuous night-and-day flight from San Francisco to New York. Flying in relays and guided at night by bonfires tended by friendly farmers along the route, the pilots flew the mail across the country in 33 hours and 21 minutes. The Post Office Department immediately arranged for the installation of lighted airways and the planes were equipped with navigation and landing lights.

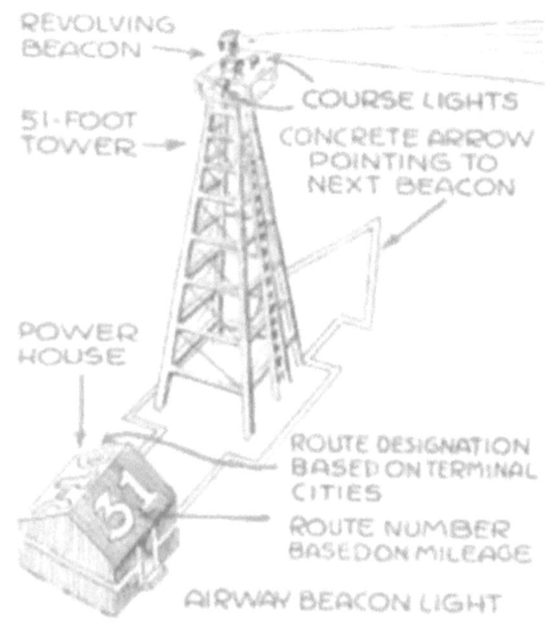

AIRWAY BEACON LIGHT

By July, 1924, a continuous chain of lighted airway beacons marked the air mail route from coast to coast. Lighted landing fields were established at 250-mile intervals and through transcontinental air mail service, with night-and-day flying, was an accomplished fact.

♦ ♦ ♦

13

AMERICA'S FIRST ALL-METAL TRANSPORT

We have spoken of the fact that in the early twenties aircraft designers were hesitant about attempting to overcome the prejudice of aviators against the internally braced monoplane design. However, there was one young man who had never been timid about the idea. He was a tall, scholarly fellow who, as a youngster, was designing and flying model planes before the Wright Brothers made their first flight. Like the Wrights he was the son of a minister. This young man, William Bushnell Stout by name, worked his way through the University of Minnesota by firing a furnace. After graduation he worked for a newspaper and edited a boys' page, one of the first in America that gave complete directions for building model airplanes.

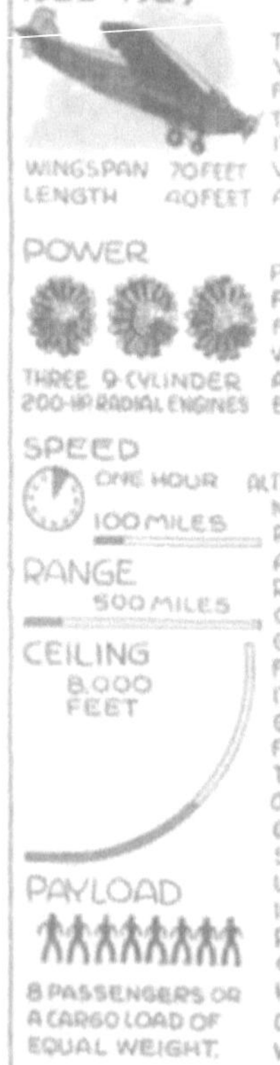

With the outbreak of World War I, Bill Stout became technical adviser to the Aircraft Board in Washington. His first advice to the aviation experts there was to scrap all existing designs and build a streamlined monoplane with an internally braced wing without struts or wires. They said it could not be done. Bill promptly sat down and drew workable plans for such a ship.

Eventually the Government bought Bill Stout's design and with the money he set up his own engineering laboratory in Detroit, Michigan. He decided that wood and fabric were not suitable to stand the strain required in a modern plane. His first all-metal plane, a Navy torpedo bomber, flew successfully in test flights, but a Navy pilot wrecked it on its official trial. The Navy would not order another one, so Bill had to raise more money. He got it and built America's first all-metal transport plane. It carried eight passengers in addition to the two-man crew. Bill knew it was a good plane and he was satisfied with it, but he did not want to be a manufacturer. He wanted instead to stay at his engineering work, so he sold his airplane company to Henry Ford, and the famous Stout-designed, Ford tri-motor, "Tin Goose" was born.

Just about the time the Ford tri-motors were proving themselves in tests an important law was passed by Congress. It was the Kelly Air Commerce Act of 1925. It authorized the Post Office Department to contract with private firms to fly the air mail routes maintained by the Department of Commerce. This law was designed to encourage private capital to enter the aviation field, with the objective of carrying not only mail but passengers. In February, 1926, officials of one of the newly formed air transport firms proudly watched their first big air transport plane take off from the Detroit airport. The big plane was a Stout-designed, all-metal Ford, the first of a series of airliners that were destined to make aviation history.

WATER-COOLED IN-LINE ENGINE

By the end of 1926, there were sixteen air transport operators holding air mail contracts. Most of the flying was still done in single-engined planes. Up to that time the weight of the big water-cooled engines in multi-engined transports left little to spare for pay loads. It was not until the development of the radial engine that commercial aviation really started.

The in-line engine required a long, heavy crankshaft with sections for each cylinder. This required that separate crankshaft bearings be used for each cylinder. The whole crankshaft assembly was heavy and cumbersome. When extra cylinders were added, the engine's weight increased and it became longer. In the radial engine a single crankshaft hearing was used.

AIR-COOLED RADIAL ENGINE

The radial air-cooled engine immediately showed many advantages over the in-line, water-cooled engines of that time. The use of aluminum in its construction made it lighter. It was cooled by allowing air to rush through finely spaced fins on cylinder heads and barrels. The weight of the cooling liquid (water) and the pump and mechanism to circulate it was avoided.

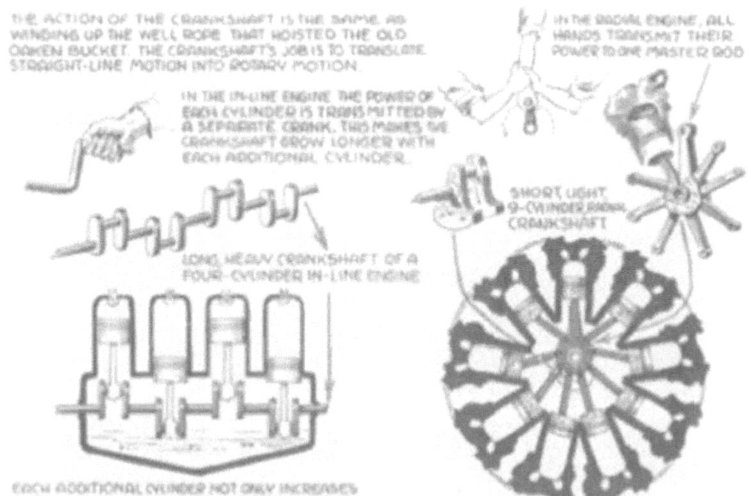
THE ACTION OF THE CRANKSHAFT IS THE SAME AS WINDING UP THE WELL ROPE THAT HOISTED THE OLD OAKEN BUCKET. THE CRANKSHAFT'S JOB IS TO TRANSLATE STRAIGHT-LINE MOTION INTO ROTARY MOTION.
IN THE IN-LINE ENGINE THE POWER OF EACH CYLINDER IS TRANSMITTED BY A SEPARATE CRANK. THIS MAKES THE CRANKSHAFT GROW LONGER WITH EACH ADDITIONAL CYLINDER.
LONG, HEAVY CRANKSHAFT OF A FOUR-CYLINDER IN-LINE ENGINE
IN THE RADIAL ENGINE, ALL HANDS TRANSMIT THEIR POWER TO ONE MASTER ROD
SHORT, LIGHT 9-CYLINDER RADIAL CRANKSHAFT
EACH ADDITIONAL CYLINDER NOT ONLY INCREASES THE LENGTH OF THE CRANKSHAFT, BUT IT ALSO MAKES IT NECESSARY TO CONSTRUCT A HEAVIER BASE TO SUPPORT THE CYLINDERS, CRANKSHAFT, AND CRANKSHAFT BEARINGS.
IN THE RADIAL ENGINE, THE POWER OF ALL CYLINDERS IS TRANSLATED INTO ROTARY MOTION BY RODS CONNECTED TO THE MASTER ROD, WHICH TURNS THE SHORT CRANKSHAFT.

◆ ◆ ◆

14

BETTER POWER FOR AMERICA'S AIRPLANES

LINDBERGH'S RYAN MONOPLANE *SPIRIT OF ST. LOUIS*

The Wright Brothers' first airplane engine had weighed 170 pounds and had produced 12 horsepower. It had used twenty-five per cent of its energy propelling itself. With the introduction of the air-cooled, radial engine twenty years later, a pound and a half of engine had been made to produce one horsepower. Thus the new 350-pound radial engine of 200 horsepower put all but a fraction of weight into load-carrying power.

While we are discussing horsepower, it might be well to find out just what we mean by the term. In connection with steam and gasoline engines it is used for the reason that the horse had for years been man's most common power plant. One horsepower represents the power ascribed to a heavy dray horse in the days of horse-drawn vehicles. This "standard" one-horse's-power includes the three factors, time, weight, and distance, or the length of time it takes to move a certain weight a certain distance. One horsepower in these factors amounts to the ability to lift 33,000 pounds one foot in one minute. Actual brake tests, where an experimental engine shows its ability to lift a certain number of pounds so high in one minute, gives the engineer a series of tables to be used in designing other engines. Each cylinder produces an equal share of the engine's total horsepower. Thus each cylinder of the nine-cylinder, 200-horsepower, Wright radial engine produced slightly over 22 horsepower, or eight more than the entire four cylinders of the Wright Brothers' 1903 engine.

With the introduction of the first practical, light-weight, air-cooled, radial engine, American aviation underwent a great change for the better.

The Lawrance-designed Wright J engines promptly began to put a long succession of famous fliers and famous airplanes in the books for one record after another. The Stout-designed Ford tri-motor transport plane was powered with Wright J3 radials. The J3 was adapted for use by the United States Navy and led the Navy to discontinue entirely its use of liquid-cooled power plants in favor of air-cooled radial engines for all its service airplanes. Wright J4 engines powered the flight of Admiral Richard E. Byrd and Floyd Bennett over the North Pole in 1926. Tony Fokker, who had designed Germany's fighters in World War I, began to make records with his American-built planes powered with Wright radials.

With the arrival of a suitable engine, fliers all over the country began to think of the Raymond Orteig prize of $25,000 for the first nonstop flight from New York to Paris. This offer had been standing since 1919. Admiral Byrd was ready to try for it when a slim, quiet, young air mail pilot hopped off from Long Island, N. Y. Flying a Ryan monoplane powered with a Wright J5 radial, this young fellow flew the Atlantic nonstop to land, some thirty-three hours and thirty-nine minutes later, in Paris with the quiet announcement, "I am Charles Lindbergh."

♦ ♦ ♦

15

RECORD-MAKING FOKKER TRI-MOTOR TRANSPORT PLANE

The best fighter planes used by the Germans in World War I were not of German design. They were designed and built under the supervision of a young man from Holland. Tony Fokker had offered his airplane designs to his native Holland. They were refused. In turn, Fokker tried to interest the British, French, and Belgians in his airplanes, but none of them took him seriously. Just before World War I, the Germans "tied up" Fokker with a contract that kept him practically their prisoner until the war was over.

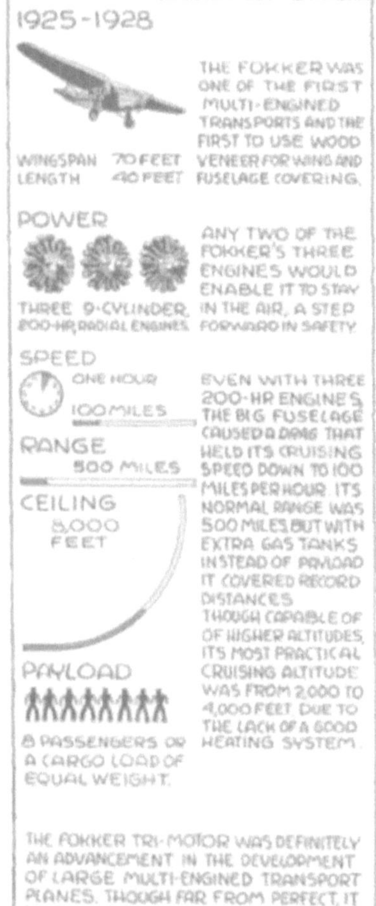

After the Armistice, Fokker fled from Germany with much of his equipment and established himself in an airplane factory in his homeland. The United States bought some of his airplanes, and in 1923 he established an aircraft factory in this country.

In April of the same year, two Army lieutenants, Oakley Kelly and John Macready, flying a Fokker T-2 powered by a *Liberty* engine, set a world's endurance record by remaining in the air for thirty-six hours. Later, in the same Fokker, they flew nonstop from Long Island to California at a speed of nearly one hundred miles an hour. In 1925, Fokker began building his famous Fokker tri-motor transport plane.

Among the first private firms that were successful in winning an air mail contract was the Colonial Air Transport, operating between New York and Boston. This airline was started in 1925 by a young ex-Navy flyer named Juan Trippe, descendant of an old New England whaling family. Young Trippe's airline used a small fleet of Tony Fokker's tri-motor transport planes. In December, 1925, Juan Trippe, Tony Fokker, Harry Bruno, and George Pond, the pilot, climbed into one of the Fokker tri-motors on what Trippe called a survey flight. The "survey" included some flying around the Florida coast and climaxed with a record nonstop flight from Miami, to Havana, Cuba.

The idea behind Juan Trippe's "survey" flight to Florida and Havana was to extend Colonial Air Transport's route from Boston to Florida, then on southward. His board of directors could not see his point, so Trippe left Colonial. In a matter of weeks he had rounded up a few ex-war flier friends with money, and had organized his own airline under the title, Pan American Airways. Before it was completely set up Trippe had a contract to fly the mail from Key West, Florida, to Havana, Cuba. That was in 1928. From that time on, Juan Trippe's Pan American Airways continued to move just as fast as it had in its first few weeks of organization. Less than two years after the first Key West-Havana flight, Pan American was flying the mail to the Argentine.

♦ ♦ ♦

16

AIR TRANSPORT GROWS

While Tony Fokker was producing his famous tri-motor transports for budding airlines like Juan Trippe's Pan American Airways, Admiral Byrd and three companions had flown a tri-motored Fokker to France. Clarence Chamberlain and Charles Levine flew a Bellanca radial-powered monoplane to Germany; Army Lieutenants Maitland and Hegenberger flew 2,400 miles nonstop from Oakland, California, to Honolulu, Hawaii, in a radial-powered Fokker; Amelia Earhart and Wilmer Stultz flew a Fokker from Newfoundland to England. Amelia thus became the first woman to cross the Atlantic in an airplane. Later she was to fly the Atlantic alone.

Tony Fokker's tri-motors and Wright radial engines predominated in the famous flights of the late twenties, but other American planes and engines were coming into prominence. The first Wright 200-horsepower radial engine was called the *Whirlwind.* It was soon followed by a more powerful Wright radial, the 400-horsepower *Cyclone.* At the same time the Pratt & Whitney organization of Hartford, Connecticut, made the 425-horsepower air-cooled *Wasp* radial engine. Wright *Cyclones* and Pratt & Whitney *Wasps* were destined to power American airplanes for many years to come.

During 1927 and 1928 the map of the United States showed a continually increasing number of lines marked "Air Mail Route." In 1926, the sixteen companies holding air mail contracts flew about 1,700,000 air miles. Much of this mileage was flown in single-engined, open-cockpit airplanes. Mail was the principal source of revenue. The few passengers who first braved the rigors of early air transport either rode on mail sacks or in small, cramped cockpits. Pilots and Operation men alike frankly admitted they were not keen about carrying passengers.

The Boeing Aircraft Company of Seattle, Washington, set up the Boeing Air Transport and took over the operation of the air mail service from Chicago to San Francisco. National Air Transport handled the Chicago-New York route, to complete the transcontinental route. Jack Frye and others established an air mail and transport service between Los Angeles, California, and Phoenix, Arizona. Western Air Express operated between Los Angeles and Salt Lake City, Utah. A number of short lines operating routes from the Great Lakes and down through the south were soon to be merged to create American Airlines.

In 1928, an air traveler making an extensive trip would be likely to fly in seven or eight different types of planes. He might step into a Fokker tri-motor, change to a single-engined Boeing, ride for some distance in a Ford tri-motor or a Whirlwind-powered *Travel Air*, and finish his trip in a Curtiss *Carrier Pigeon*. The planes usually flew low, at between one and two thousand feet. Here the air was usually rough and a good percentage of air travelers were troubled with airsickness. The planes landed every few hundred miles to refuel. They were noisy and heated only by exhaust gases from the engines, which usually furnished more sickly fumes than heat. Little food, if any, was served, and a coast-to-coast journey took thirty-three hours.

Though 1926 was the official start of American air transport, the first two years of its existence were years of experimentation. It was not until the country's imagination had been fired by the flights of Lindbergh, Byrd, Chamberlain, and others that air transport emerged from its experimental stage. By 1927 the bigger minds in airline services had realized that the time was coming when provisions must be made to carry passengers on a large scale. It was not until 1928, with the arrival of powerful radial engines and better airplane designs, that air transport began to show real prospects. It was two years after the first beginnings of air transport that John Monk Saunders, the author, paid over $400 for an air passage from Los Angeles to New York, and became the first transcontinental air passenger.

Although its aircraft production had been mainly for the Army and Navy, the Boeing Aircraft Company also was in the air transport business through its Chicago-San Francisco air mail route. Boeing's inventive genius was turned to air transport problems and created, first, the Boeing 40-B4 four-passenger and mail plane. Then came the big twelve-passenger, radial-powered, tri-motor plane, called the "Pioneer Pullman of the Air." This ship, Boeing 80-A, helped to reduce the coast-to-coast transport time to twenty-seven hours. When the 80-A was introduced the Boeing Air Transport and the National Air Transport had been merged to form United Air Lines, the first transcontinental airline.

With air transport five years old, by 1930 the speed of planes was only about 100 miles per hour. Engineers and transport men agreed that the air transport plane must be faster. The planes of that day still had a considerable amount of external bracing and many of them were biplanes with strut and wire wing bracings. This caused the drag that was holding down the speed of the transport. Many of these planes had so many bracings that they whistled as they flew. To make a profit, the air transport operators had to have faster, quieter, and yet more comfortable airplanes. They must also be more easily maintained.

In 1921, Boeing came up with a plane that, while not the final answer to the air transport problem, was to point the way to the modern all-metal, monoplane type of air transports. This plane was the Boeing *Monomail.* The *Monomail* was big, fast, and comfortable, and it carried a big pay load. It was the first practical low-wing, all-metal transport to be put into service in this country. It carried five passengers, their baggage, and 1,750 pounds of mail or cargo, at a cruising speed of 140 miles per hour. The *Monomail* was the sensation of air transport in 1931, and set the pace for future transport planes.

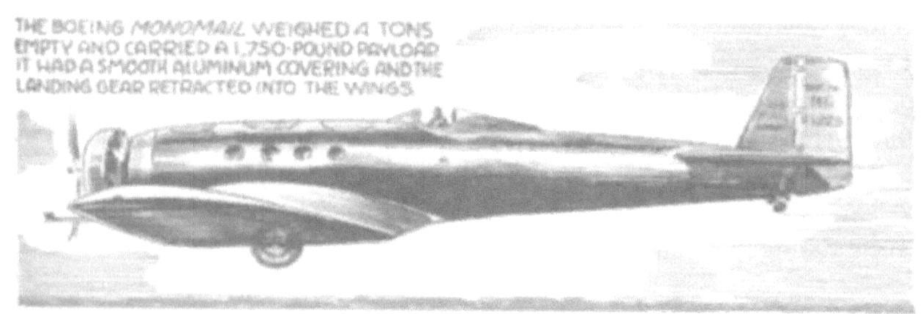

♦ ♦ ♦

17

DONALD DOUGLAS'DREAM COMES TRUE

The Boeing people, though pleased with the reception and performance of the *Monomail*, knew that the single-engine plane was not the final answer. If the engine failed, the plane must land. If the plane was over rough or mountainous country, forced landings meant danger. A big plane must have two engines, one of which could keep the plane flying if the other failed. Boeing went to work with this in mind.

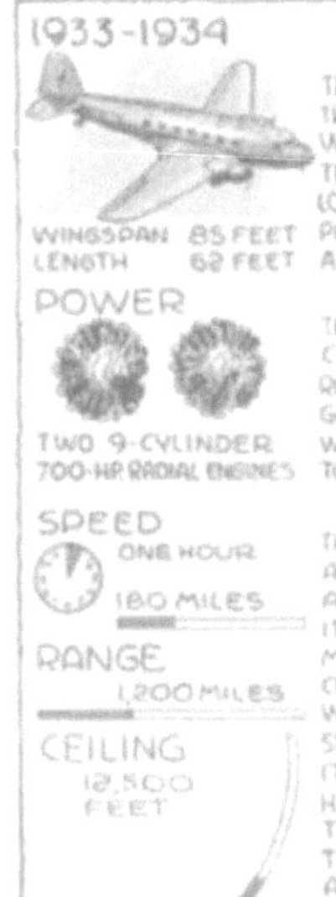

Near Los Angeles, the young man who had been dreaming of big commercial transport planes since the Wright Brothers' trials at Fort Meyer, also was thinking of two-engined transports that could fly on one engine. From the time Donald Douglas' *World Cruisers* had circled the globe, his aircraft had grown larger and larger. His orders, however, were for Army, Navy, and Coast Guard planes; not for great commercial airliners.

Although Donald Douglas had achieved a great deal of international fame as the result of the round-the-world flight and was highly respected in military circles, few other people knew him. A quiet, industrious young man, he had put all his earnings back into his business and had continued to work on his dream of big, roomy, smooth-flying airliners. He visualized air transport flying from coast to coast and from country to country in a great network of airlines that would link the whole world.

On a hot, dry day in the summer of 1933, in Winslow, Arizona, a new two-engined transport took off from one of the highest airports on the Transcontinental & Western Airways route. Gaining altitude, the pilot cut off one of its two engines, then flew more than 200 miles over the Rockies to Albuquerque, New Mexico. Returning, the pilot cut off one engine on the take-off. With one *Cyclone* radial roaring, the transport took off easily and climbed steadily. The first Douglas DC-1 transport had proved itself and a dream had come true.

The DC-l was an experimental model of the new Douglas two-engined luxury air transport plane. On the night of February 18, 1934, six months after the first DC-l was tested over the Rockies near Winslow, a new Cyclone-powered Douglas took off from Los Angeles for Newark,

New Jersey. This plane was the first of the famous DC-2's. It was flown by Jack Frye of TWA (Transcontinental & Western Airways) and Captain Eddie Rickenbacker of Eastern Air Lines. They roared into Newark ahead of a snowstorm which had blotted out all the airports along the route, and were three hours ahead of schedule for a new transcontinental record of 13 hours, 4 minutes. This flight made obsolete all existing transport planes.

♦ ♦ ♦

18

SAFETY IN FLIGHT

The new Douglas DC-2 transport plane combined all the knowledge of thirty years of flight. In the early "thirties" air transport began to come into its own. Plane-to-ground radio was put into use. The radio range, or radio beam, pioneered by "Shorty" Schroeder with Henry Ford in 1927, was guiding our airliners on their course. The radio beam flashed the Morse code letters "A" and "N" along the flight path of the airliner. The dot-dash of the "A" signal was flashed on one side of the route and the dash-dot of the "N" signal was on the other. In the center of the flight path the two signals blended into a steady hum. This hum notified the pilot that he was "on course." Regardless of fog, rain, or darkness the pilot got his course through his earphones.

The application of the gyroscope to aircraft instruments was a great step in the advancement of flying. First experimented with by Lawrence Sperry in the early days of the airplane, the constant action of the gyroscope was used to register the changes of attitude of aircraft in flight. It was first used in the Turn and Bank Indicator, then in the *Gyro-Horizon* and *Directional Gyro.* Power-driven gyros constantly whirled in the direction in which they were set. They were attached to dials on the instrument panel and to the plane itself. The position or attitude of the gyro was indicated on the dial in relation to the attitude of the airplane. As the plane changed, the constantly spinning gyro remained in its correct attitude. The gyro position and the position of the plane shown on the dial told the pilot the actual attitude of the plane in the air so that he could correct in relation to the true position indicated by the gyro. This allowed the pilot to keep his plane on a true compass course and in the proper flight attitude without having to see the horizon. Thus a pilot could fly through fog or total darkness with both ease and safety.

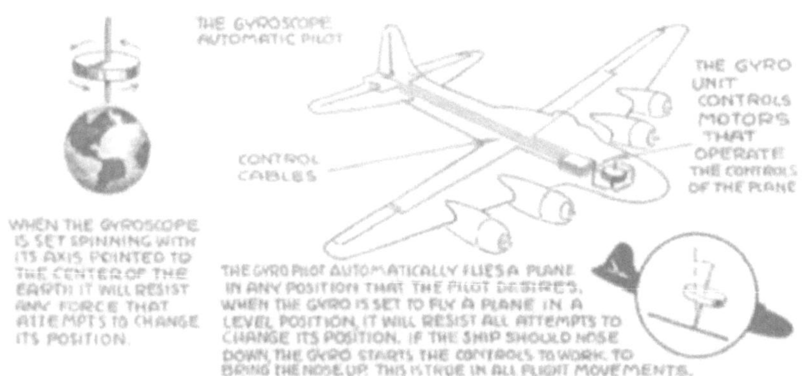

The gyro instruments soon proved their value and were installed in the cockpits of transport planes the world over. The Sperry Gyropilot then was perfected. This remarkable instrument, based on the gyroscope movement, was developed actually to manipulate automatically the controls of even the largest airplane, keeping it directly on the desired course and leaving the human pilots free for their many other duties.

In 1933, Wiley Post flew around the world alone, but the Gyropilot piloted the *Winnie Mae* over most of the route. This relieved the fatigue of constant flying and allowed Wiley to keep a continual check on his maps. His successful use of the automatic pilot soon caused its adoption by most of the major airlines of the country.

Thus, with the aid of the radio beam, better flight instruments, special octane gasoline, two-way radio, sound-proofing, wheel brakes, and adjustable pitch propellers, the airlines of America were fast emerging into a safe and comfortable means of travel.

While the DC-2 was coming into prominence in the air transport field, Boeing engineers had gone on with their idea of a two-engined plane and had built an all-metal bomber for the Army.

In building the two-engined, all-metal B-9, Boeing engineers learned how to build another plane with a more peaceful purpose. This ship was the famous Boeing 247-D commercial transport plane. The 247-D was an all-metal, low-wing monoplane, powered with two 550-horsepower Pratt & Whitney Wasp radial engines. It had a top speed of 200 miles per hour and a cruising speed of 180 miles per hour. It was America's first three-mile-a-minute air transport plane.

In designing the speedy 247-D, the Boeing did not forget the comfort of the passengers. The plane was fully heated and ventilated. Its seats were deeply upholstered and had reclining backs. There were broad windows at each chair. There were dome lights and individual reading lamps; and the plane was equipped with a tiny galley and a complete lavatory. Insulation kept the 247-D quiet and comfortable in any sort of weather.

The 247-D carried ten passengers, a pilot, co-pilot, and stewardess, plus baggage and mail. It was first put into service by the United Air Lines in 1933, on their coast-to-coast route. Incidentally, it was United who had introduced to the airlines the third member of the air transport's crew, the stewardess. The pretty young stewardesses were all trained nurses. They looked after air-sick passengers, served food en route, and looked after the comfort of the air travelers.

BOEING 247 TRANSPORT

POWERED WITH TWO 550-HP PRATT & WHITNEY RADIAL ENGINES, THE 247 CRUISED AT 180 MILES PER HOUR. ITS TEN PASSENGERS RODE IN DEEPLY CUSHIONED SEATS WITH RECLINING BACKS. ITS WELL-VENTILATED, HEATED CABIN WAS SOUND-PROOFED TO DEADEN THE ROAR OF THE ENGINES, AND THE PASSENGERS RODE IN QUIET COMFORT.

♦ ♦ ♦

19

LUXURY AIRLINERS AND SKYSLEEPERS MAKE AIR TRAVEL AN ACCEPTED FACT

With the Boeing 247's, United Air Lines in 1933 cut the coast-to-coast air trip to twenty-two hours. As DC-2's and the fast two-engined Lockheed *Electras* were speeding up air transport schedules on the airlines throughout the country, differences arose between the government and some air transport firms over mail contracts. The result was the cancellation in February, 1934, of all air mail contracts.

The air mail revenue was the life of the air transport operators and the cancellation of the mail contracts suddenly darkened their future. An attempt to put the transportation of air mail into the hands of the United States Army resulted in a tragic failure. This was due mainly to the unfamiliarity of Army pilots with air mail routes and their lack of proper equipment. In June, 1934, the air mail was turned back to the airlines.

The return of the air mail contracts to private operators

saw the introduction of the new Douglas DC-3. This was the plane that brought Donald Douglas' dream to complete fulfilment. His big, all-metal, low-wing, two-engined DC-3 completely revolutionized air transport. By 1935, the name Douglas had come to mean fast, comfortable, and safe air transport.

The Douglas DC-3 was produced in 21-passenger day planes, 14-passenger de luxe *Skylounges*, and 14-passenger *Skysleepers*. The DC-3 put "sleeper planes" on an acceptable basis. Coast-to-coast schedules were cut to three stops and an overnight trip. Fares were cut in half and air travel became an accepted fact.

THE SIKORSKY S-42, PATHFINDER OF THE PACIFIC
HAD A WINSPAN OF 118 FEET AND WAS 64 FEET LONG

♦ ♦ ♦

20

PAN AMERICAN CLIPPERS CONQUER PACIFIC SKIES

While the DC-3's were cutting to an overnight hop the air journey from coast to coast, Captain Eddie Rickenbacker had pushed his Eastern Air Lines from New York to Miami, Florida. Here it connected with Juan Trippe's Pan American Airways. By this time Trippe's Pan American *Clipper* planes regularly were covering a route from Miami down through the West Indies to Rio de Janeiro, Brazil, and to Buenos Aires in the Argentine. At Buenos Aires Pan American Airways connected with Harold R. Harris' Pan American-Grace Airways to complete a route over the Andes and back up the west coast of South America.

The story of Harold Harris and his airway is a book in itself. Harris, a veteran flier of World War I, had been an Army test pilot. In 1922 he became the first member of the "Caterpillar Club" when he used a parachute to escape from a plane which had failed. Later, as a crop-dusting pilot in Peru, he visualized and founded the Pan American-Grace air route.

By the time Juan Trippe's Pan American Clippers were flying over every country in Central and South America, his active mind was busy planning another "survey." Though his company at that time was operating the world's largest airline, Trippe was planning new worlds to conquer.

Pan American had been using Igor Sikorsky's four-engined flying boats on his route to Rio and Buenos Aires, and Trippe sent one of them, with veteran Edwin Misick in command, on a "survey" flight westward across the Pacific.

On November 22, 1935, Pan American Airways' *China Clipper* took off from San Francisco Bay on its first scheduled trans-Pacific flight to Manila, Philippine Islands. One hundred years before, to the day, the first Yankee clipper ship had sailed into the same bay. Twenty-five years before, a young man had made America's first trans-Pacific flight—a flight of 33 miles from the California shore to Catalina Island. The 26-ton *China Clipper* heading into its 8,000-mile trans-Pacific flight was a Martin 130 flying boat built by Glenn L. Martin, the young fellow of the Catalina flight. In just 59 hours and 48 minutes of flying time the first *China Clipper* landed in Manila Bay.

♦ ♦ ♦

21

PAN AMERICAN CLIPPER INAUGURATES AMERICA'S FIRST TRANSATLANTIC AIR TRANSPORT SERVICE

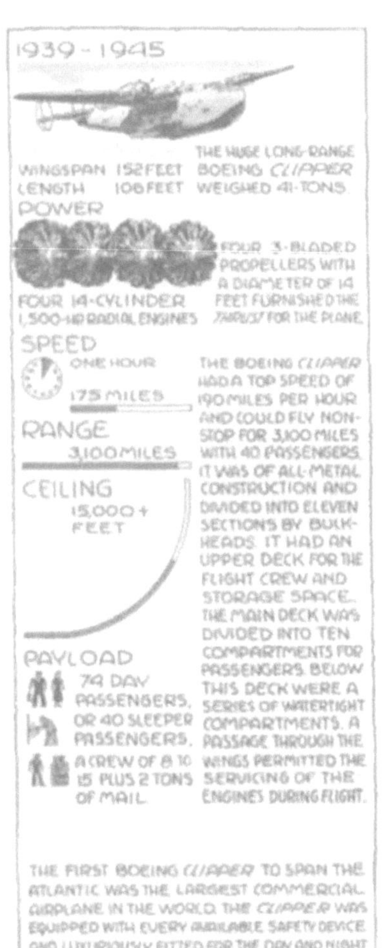

With the sweep of its wings the first *China Clipper* ripped out weeks of slow surface travel to the rich markets of the Far East. By 1936 a trip from this country to China was measured by a matter of sixty or seventy flight hours instead of by weeks.

It was not the big clipper planes alone that built the far-flung Pan American Airways. Juan Trippe visualized his world airways system and then picked the finest experts in every field to carry out his plans. Former diplomats covered the proposed routes long before the Clippers flew them. There was, of course, no freedom of the air. No plane could fly over a foreign country without permission. Trippe's emissaries had to get franchises. Germany, France, Britain, and Holland were after franchises in South America too. There, as in the Far East, they got the rights to fly, not by government pressure, but by selling aviation as a valuable business asset to any nation.

Once Trippe had his franchises, he sent experts to explore and lay out routes. They carved airports out of jungles and Arctic wastes, and in places where no white man ever had penetrated. The supply problems overcome and the engineering marvels performed by Trippe's advance men would furnish plots for a dozen movie thrillers. In laying out the bases at Wake and Guam on the Pacific route, more than one million separate items were bought, shipped, and installed before the first *China Clipper* took off from San Francisco.

Pan American's map added another blue line after the Pacific route was under way. This time it was to Alaska, and another distant travel time could be reckoned in flight hours rather than ocean days.

Then came the Atlantic and the giant Boeing 314 Pan American *Clippers.*

Boeing achieved such excellent results with its two-engined planes that its engineers went on to plan four-engined super-planes. When Juan

Trippe wanted a plane for his Atlantic service, Boeing was ready with the 41-ton Boeing 314. The 314 *Atlantic Clippers* carried 74 passengers and boasted of compartments that could be converted into berths, dressing rooms, a dining salon, and a real kitchen for serving hot meals aloft. On May 20, 1939, just twenty years after the first transatlantic flight of the Navy NC's, the *Atlantic Clipper* took off on the trip that inaugurated Pan American Airways service to Europe. Juan Trippe's dream was reaching around the world.

♦ ♦ ♦

22

PRIVATE PLANES

In the very early days of aviation, before the start of World War I, most of the airplanes, with the exception of a few military ships, were sold to private owners. Those buyers were either barnstormers or wealthy sportsmen. Some advertising in national magazines even tried to create sales, for private planes. This activity ceased with the beginning of the war in 1914, and owners turned their planes over to the Government for training purposes.

At the end of the war there were hundreds of young men who had learned to fly. This situation brought about a considerable amount of private flying. However, most of the ex-service men bought surplus war equipment, such as the Curtiss *Jenny*, so that there was not a large market for the manufacturers of new private planes.

Following the Lindbergh flight to Paris and other spectacular aviation achievements, the American public really became air-conscious. It was at that time that the private plane came into its own.

People began to find that airplanes were of practical value, and business firms began to use them in various ways. Sales and service representatives could cover vast areas in a short time. Essential equipment could be carried swiftly by airplanes over stretches of country which before had been almost inaccessible. Ranchers used planes to cover far-flung ranges. Explorers and scientists alike used the airplane to search for hidden treasure and precious minerals in spots which before had been impossible to reach by land transportation.

All this activity brought about the development of more comfortable cabin planes and led to a demand for large and small private ships. The small, light plane field expanded with amazing speed once there was a demand. In the late twenties Aëronca, Taylor, and Piper began to bring out safe, comfortable, and inexpensive planes. By the middle thirties flying schools and private landing fields were a common sight throughout America.

As the light planes became popular, the training of private pilots developed into a big business. Flying lessons became an important source of income to aviators who heretofore had operated their little airfields on the revenue derived from sightseeing hops and an occasional charter trip. Student pilots became logical prospects forlight planes and the more successful flying schools became sales agencies for the aircraft manufacturers. Students became expert fliers and graduated to instructors' jobs. A number of these young instructors in turn bought light planes and started flying schools of their own. Thus, light plane flying spread like wildfire over the country.

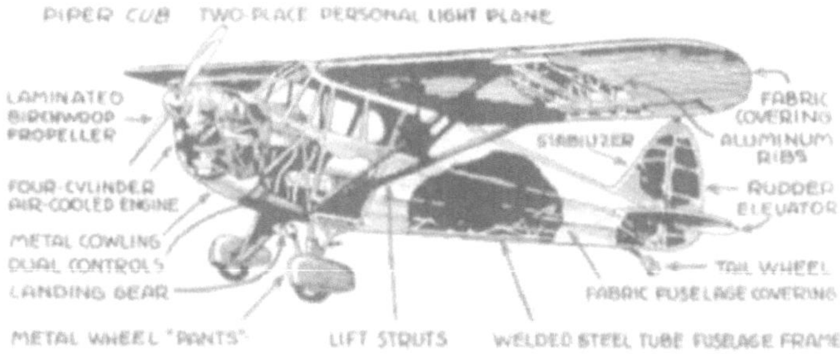

The light planes of the late thirties were mainly high-wing monoplanes. They were powered with light, air-cooled engines and were so designed that they had a high factor of safety. They were sturdily built and easy to fly. The average student was able to solo after eight or ten lessons, though real flying ability came only through constant practice. Light planes cost from $1,500 to $2,000. Many of them were equipped with accessories such as heaters, radios, navigation lights, and flight instruments. All of them had comfortably upholstered, enclosed cabins. In the years just before World War II light plane flying for business and pleasure was an accepted mode of travel for boys and girls as well as men and women of all ages.

♦ ♦ ♦

23

SUPERCHARGERS AND SUPER-AIRLINERS

High above the earth, 14,000 to 20,000 feet, lies a region of smooth air called the substratosphere.

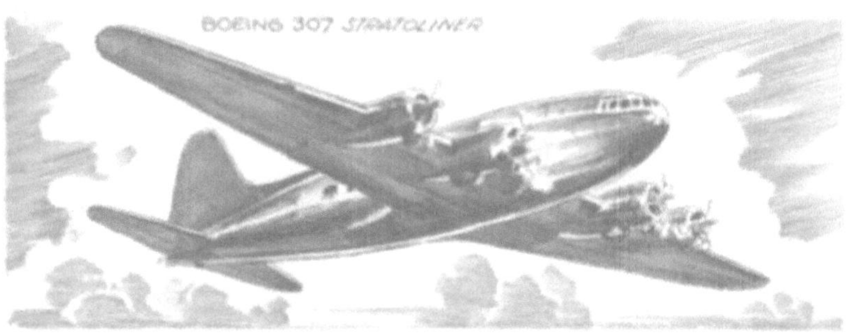

Pioneer fliers had reached this region years before, but its thin, rare air made life and movement impossible. Men had long looked to this smooth-air region as the ideal flight path—a path without rough air, or fog, or storm to slow their progress. But both they and their engines needed plenty of air for operation.

It was not until 1939, when Dr. Sanford Moss invented the turbo-supercharger, that high engine performance at altitudes above 30,000 feet became a matter of fact. The turbo-supercharger, a simple machine driven by the force of the engine exhausts, pumped air into the engines to give them sea-level pressure at high altitudes. This took care of the engines in the smooth-air substratosphere regions.

Next came the human element. Human beings, like engines, cannot live without sufficient air. This brought about the development of the supercharged cabin for airplanes. In 1936 "Tommy" Tomlinson, a brilliant ex-Navy flier, started making experimental substratosphere flights for TWA in a specially designed plane. He found that the speed of a properly equipped airplane would increase some 36 per cent at 30,000 feet. At the same time Army engineers were experimenting with a Lockheed plane having a supercharged cabin.

The Boeing Company, working in co-operation with Tomlinson, Transcontinental and Western Airways, and Pan American, developed the Boeing 307. The 307 was a big all-metal, low-wing monoplane with a pressurized, high-altitude cabin, which made possible flight at altitudes up to 20,000 feet. This was accomplished in a manner similar to that used in supercharging the engines. Engine-driven superchargers pumped air into the cabin-ventilating system and the atmosphere in the plane was kept at normal low-level pressure regardless of how high the plane flew. The Boeing 307 *Stratoliner* was put into service by TWA and Pan American Airways in 1940 and marked a tremendous step forward in the speed and comfort of modern air travel.

In 1941, fifteen years after the operation of the nation's airlines had been turned over to private firms, air transport was approaching perfection. The first single-engined, two-passenger mail planes, cruising at 100 miles per hour, took thirty-three hours to make the coast-to-coast trip. Now giant luxury airliners were doing it in fifteen hours. In contrast to the frequent stops of the low-flying plane of the early days, the high-flying air transports of 1941 were making the journey with only three stops. Where the air traveler of the twenties rode in an uncomfortable seat in a cold, gas-smelling plane, and was lucky if he got a box lunch, the modern passenger rode in luxuriously upholstered chairs in a heated salon, and dined on hot fried chicken or steak with all the "trimmings."

Even more significant was the change in flight and safety aids. No longer did the pilot fly with his eyes on the railroad tracks and the family wash on the line below. Radio communication with the ground, continual weather information, and precision navigation and flight instruments changed all that and brought safety to air transport.

With domestic airline routes covering America from coast to coast and from border to border, and with the wings of Pan American's *Clippers* casting their shadows over 75,000 miles of the earth's surface, the Japs struck at Pearl Harbor.

♦ ♦ ♦

24

AIR POWER FOR WORLD WAR II

In September, 1939, when the first Nazi Stukas screamed down on Poland, we produced only 117 military aircraft. Our Army Air Corps could muster only some 21,000 officers and men, and the Navy could not boast of even that many. Neither the Army nor Navy had more than a thousand planes each. That meant all types: trainers, transport planes, and fighters. The Nazi *Luftwaffe* at that time was composed of more than a million men and 15,000 warplanes, and the Japanese had many more planes than we ever had thought they could build. This was the beginning not only of World War II, but of *Air War I.*

This was not the first time that the United States got off to a late start. The same thing was true in World War I. Nevertheless, with typical American confidence, we thought we could do it again. Consequently, in 1940, we set as our goal the building of 50,000 warplanes.

We lost the first rounds of the fight while we were getting started. In the South Pacific it was ten Jap planes to our one; at Wake Island, four obsolete Marine Corps fighters flew gallantly to meet a hundred of the foe. At Pearl Harbor hangars full of planes were caught on the ground. At Corregidor there was a cry of "No planes!"

But a typical American once said, "We have not yet begun to fight." As in World War I, our military and industrial aviation leaders "rolled up their sleeves" and began to fight. As a result, in less than three years, they produced the greatest aërial fighting force that the world ever has known.

Let us go back to 1920 and review the progress of our Army and Naval aviation up to the start of World War II. We shall find out why we were able to create unbeatable air power when the crisis came.

♦ ♦ ♦

25

NAVALAVIATION 1922-1935

From its earliest beginnings United States naval aviation made progress far out of proportion to the small amount of money appropriated by the Government. But it was a young and eager organization with a constant desire to do things—to stretch its wings. An aërial world remained unexplored and naval aviators were an inquisitive lot.

The first carrier, the *Langley*, with a complement of six airplanes, became the training ground for the young naval aviators who were to lay the foundation for the world's greatest seagoing aërial task force. While the *Langley* was primitive by today's standards, experiments with it pointed the way for the development of improved types of carrier-based fighting planes. However, the enthusiasm of the young naval aviators was not shared entirely by other Navy men based on surface craft. To them airplanes were just something to be fished out of the sea when an engine failed. It was some time before the aviators were able to convince these others of the exceptional value of planes in spotting gunfire and scouting for an enemy.

Regardless of the fact that they were the Navy's orphans, the young pioneers kept at it. They flew the crude machines available and developed tactics for carrier-based airplanes. They improved the arresting gear and solved many technical problems in ways that enabled aircraft builders to design airplanes especially suitable for use on carriers. At the same time, it was natural that flying boats should appeal to Navy men. The flight of the NC flying boats inspired the development of long-range patrol boats. Naval aviators also went ahead with experiments which were to lead to the creation of flying boats with a range of 2,000 miles and more.

While the naval aviators were busy with their early experiments on the *Langley*, the Disarmament Conference of 1922 had changed this country's plans for the construction of new battleships. However, the United States and Great Britain were permitted, by the terms of the conference agreement, each to have 135,000 tons of airplane carriers.

Two of the big cruisers under construction at that time were converted into carriers. These two, our first specifically designed-aircraft carriers, were the *Lexington* and the *Saratoga*. When commissioned in 1927, the *Lexington* and the *Saratoga* were the biggest and best aircraft carriers in the world. Weighing about 35,000 tons and capable of carrying sixty to eighty airplanes,

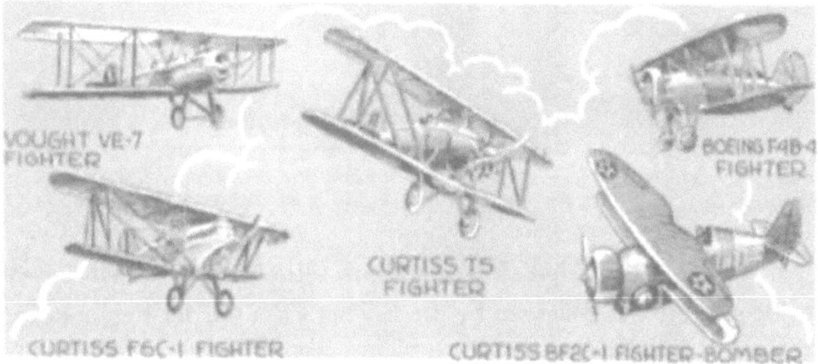

they were the fastest ships of their type afloat. The ships—the "Lex" and the "Sara," as airmen called them—became the twin mothers of carrier fighter tactics and operational techniques.

The U. S. Navy pioneered in the development of aircraft as a military weapon and spared no effort to develop it and fit it into naval organization. The *Lexington* and the *Saratoga* were the proving grounds for the ideas of our imaginative leaders of naval aviation. The lessons learned in maneuvers with the *Lexington* and *Saratoga* were well embedded in the minds of the men who were someday to command the greatest carrier task force the world has ever seen. The old *Lexington* and *Saratoga* were in the thick of the fight in the Pacific from the day after Pearl Harbor. The "Lex" went down in the gallant fight that stopped the Japs in the Coral Sea. Within two years a new and more powerful *Lexington* was hammering the Japs in the Pacific. The *Saratoga*, damaged severely several times, lived through the heroic struggle to see victory. The "Lex" and the "Sara" will always live in the hearts of the Navy's veteran airmen.

♦ ♦ ♦

26

SHIPBOARD FIGHTERS

GRUMMAN FF-1 FIGHTER

The Curtiss TS-1 was the first carrier fighter built to Navy specification. It was followed by the Boeing FB-l. Carrier fighters offered one of aviation's most difficult problems. A carrier fighter had to have a short takeoff run, necessitated by the carrier's short deck. Another requirement was a short wingspan to permit the storage of a number of planes in the limited space of the carrier's hangar deck. As a result, small light biplanes were used on the carriers for many years. The Curtiss BFC-l and BF2C-l were the first carrier-based aircraft to be equipped with retractable landing gear.

The Boeing F4B-4, though it did not have a retractable landing gear, was a very fast, all-metal fighter and was popular as a carrier-based fighter. Grumman came into the picture in 1935 with a stubby, fast, two-place fighter, the FF-1. It was highly successful, but was later re-designed as a scout plane, the SF-1. The FF-1 was the fastest fighter yet to appear in service and, after several modifications, it became the F3F-1, a design standardized by the Navy and used throughout by the carriers' fighter squadrons.

U.S. AIRCRAFT CARRIER LEXINGTON

27

BATTLESHIP OF THE AIR

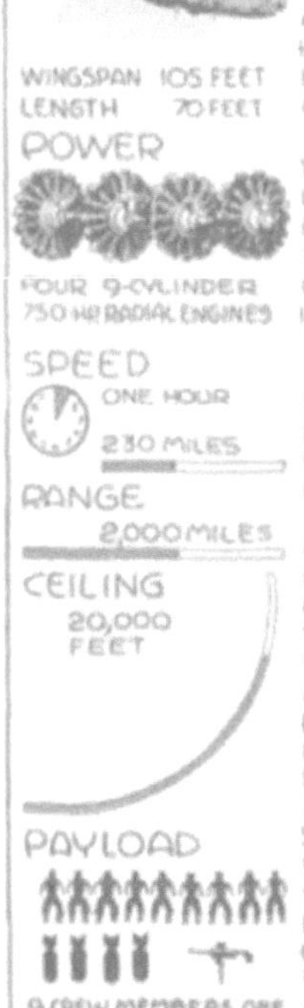

In line with its strategic policy the Army Air Corps continued to develop aviation around long-range bombardment. Long-range bombers would stop an invader far from our shores and therefore the aim of our Air Corps leaders was to develop a bomber that could be used for that purpose.

The Martin BM-1, the Barling bomber, and the Keystone LB-6, developed in the twenties, were all biplanes made of wood, metal, and fabric. What the Army airmen really wanted was an all-metal, low-wing, multi-engined bomber capable of flying far out to sea, dropping its bombs, and returning to its base on land. Naturally at that time our only thoughts were of weapons for defense and the protection of our coastline from an invader.

The Martin B-10 two-engined bomber seemed to fill the Army requirements. It was a low-wing monoplane capable of carrying a ton of bombs a thousand miles at a speed of nearly 200 miles per hour. It became the Army's standard bomber in 1934.

In the same year ten Martin B-10's, under the command of (then) Lieutenant Colonel Henry H. Arnold, made an historic flight to Alaska. This Alaskan trip was climaxed by a nonstop flight from Juneau, Alaska, to Seattle, Washington, 943 miles over water in five hours and forty minutes. Alaska's nearness became apparent and American airpower was needed to defend it. Army officials and top air strategists went to work. The answer was a call for bigger bombers with greater range, greater bomb capacity, and greater speed.

The Boeing Company, whose B-9 all-metal, low-wing, two-engined bomber had proved sensational in 1932, produced the answer to the Army's problem of 1935. The answer was the giant four-engined model 299, America's first four-engined bomber. It was a mid-wing, all-metal monoplane with a wingspan of 104 feet. With a top speed of over 250 miles per hour its performance was more than sensational.

The pioneering of unusual airplanes like the *Monomail*, the B-9, and the 247 transport were steps toward the Boeing 299. It was a courageous step from two-engined to four-engined bombers, but the Boeing

Company made it so successfully that almost instantly the United States Army Air Corps won world leadership in long-range, heavy bombardment aviation.

The exceptional speed, range, armament, and bomb capacity of the 299 quickly resulted in the dramatic name *Flying Fortress*. As the B-17 it flew across the country at 232 miles per hour. In 1938, six B-17 *Flying Fortresses* set unofficial world records for speed and range in a mass flight from Langley Field, Virginia, to Buenos Aires, Argentina, and return.

♦ ♦ ♦

28

NAVAL AVIATIONGETS READY

From 1930 to 1940 the small but efficient air arm of the United States Navy continued to make progress. Since the introduction of the radial engine, the Navy had worked closely with manufacturers of this type of power plant. All types of Navy airplanes were powered with either Wright or Pratt & Whitney air-cooled, radial engines. Many problems peculiar to naval aircraft were worked out through the close co-operation of Navy technicians and manufacturers. Corrosion-resistant metals were developed for cylinders. Stronger engine parts were introduced to withstand the stress of dive-bombing. Continual progress was made in increasing the power of the engine without increasing its weight per horsepower. Thus engine power increased from 200 horsepower in 1925 to 1,000 horsepower in 1940.

GRUMMAN F4F *WILDCAT* NAVY FIGHTER

Naval aviators, encouraged by pioneer flying officers such as Jack Towers, Marc Mitscher, Reeves, Bellinger, Read, and others, flew continually to improve their flying and tactical techniques. They flight-tested experimental planes, invented and perfected the technique of dive-bombing, and improved their skill in the difficult task of carrier operations. A young lieutenant, Frank D. Wagner, who invented dive-bombing almost twenty years ago, a rear admiral in World War II, had the satisfaction of seeing his invention, at the peak of perfection, operating with deadly effect against our enemies in the Pacific. In fact, many of the young naval aviators who fifteen years before were conducting a continual competition to see whose squadron could excel the rest in flying, dive-bombing, and gunnery, commanded the greatest naval air force in the world.

In addition to the development of carrier-based aircraft operation, the Navy perfected a catapult device which simplified the launching of planes from all types of surface vessels. In 1912 the air-minded Captain Chambers had made a successful experiment with a catapult-launching device. This device, made of material salvaged from a scrap heap, laid the foundation for catapult-launching of aircraft from surface vessels. In Captain Chambers' device the plane rested on a small car running on the catapult rail. A cylinder filled with compressed air contained a piston. When a valve was opened, the escaping air pushed the piston against the car with a force that sent the car down the catapult rail and the plane into the air.

The basic idea developed by Captain Chambers is still used in Navy catapults. In the modern device, the airplane rests on a car riding on a catapult rail which can be mounted on all types of surface craft. The rail is so constructed that it can be swung in any direction, permitting the plane to be launched into the wind. The power that shoots the catapult car and sends the plane off the rail is furnished by a five-inch shell fired in a mechanism at the rear of the rail. It was this idea of Captain Chambers' that originally gave the Navy a start on the device enabling our battleships, cruisers, and destroyers to take observation planes to sea with them. This was the idea which furnished the "eyes of the fleet" and gave admirals and captains the power to see what lay beyond the horizon.

The development of naval aviation marched step by step with the development of aircraft. The year 1940 saw the introduction of one of the best carrier-based fighters ever built, the Grumman F4F *Wildcat.* This stubby-winged craft was a radical departure from previous carrier-fighter design and became the first successful monoplane to go to sea on the carriers. Wing-flaps lowered landing speeds and shortened take-off runs. This permitted the use on the carriers of the fast fighter, since the flaps acted as brakes and reduced the plane's speed for deck landings. The F4F had a wingspan of 38 feet but this was decreased by the folding of its wings to 14 feet 6 inches. This device reduced the space necessary for storage in the carrier's hangar deck and permitted the use of additional fighters on the ship. The F4F's landing gear retracted completely into the fuselage, thus aiding in streamlining and increasing the speed of the fighter. It was powered with a 1,200-horsepower Pratt 81 Whitney air-cooled radial engine and had a speed of about 350 miles per hour.

Experiments with the use of aërial torpedoes brought about the development of the Douglas TBD-1 torpedo plane. Though not so fast as a fighter, the three-place TBD-1 *Devastator* carried a deadly torpedo load. The Douglas SBD *Dauntless* was designed for dive-bombing and was the first low-wing monoplane to be used as the standard dive-bomber on our carriers.

The Douglas SBD *Dauntless* was the first Navy dive-bomber to get into action in World War II. In fact it went into action a few minutes after the first Jap shot was fired at Pearl Harbor, on the morning of December 7th, 1941. SBD's from the carrier Enterprise, steaming toward Hawaii, were the first planes in action on that fateful morning. From that day on our war in the Pacific was one of attack. The dive-bomber is an attack weapon and the sturdy SBD's led the attack from Pearl Harbor down to Guadalcanal and on up the Pacific to the Philippines and victory.

While other types of planes were under consideration at the beginning of the war, the airplanes just discussed were the ones that bore the brunt of the fighting in the early months following the attack on Pearl Harbor. Their work in the hands of gallant Navy airmen in the heartbreaking first year of our struggle against terrific odds in the Pacific would in itself furnish material for a book many times the size of this one.

♦ ♦ ♦

29

THE U. S. NAVY'SFIRST LONG-RANGEFLYING BOATS

In the early twenties the memories of the famous transatlantic flight of the NC flying boats persisted in the minds of naval aviators. Much of the Navy's interest was centered in the Pacific, and the vision of flying boats that could quickly link Hawaii to the mainland was an enticing one.

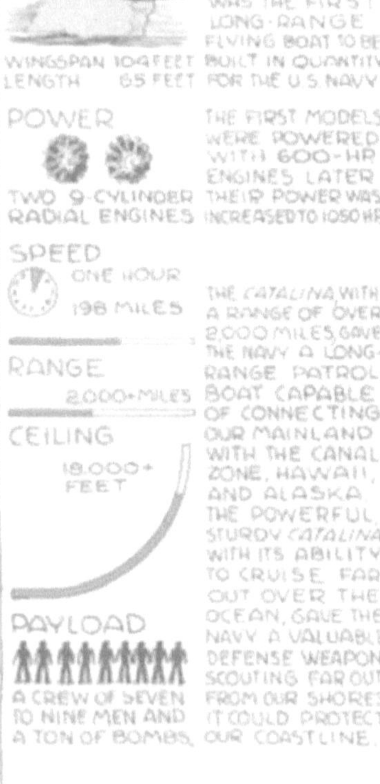

On a trial flight from San Francisco, California, to Honolulu, Hawaii, in 1925, Commander John Rogers, flying a Navy patrol plane, was forced down after twenty-five hours in the air. He was within four hundred miles of Hawaii when he landed on the sea. After drifting for nine days, Rogers was picked up by a submarine. Although the flight had failed, it had established a seaplane record of over 1,800 miles, and the trail was blazed.

It was the development of the famous Consolidated PBY flying boats that eventually put our West Coast within twenty-four hours' flying distance of Hawaii. You will remember the Army officer who had charge of our first air mail service back in 1918—Major Reuben H. Fleet. Major Fleet resigned from the service in

1922 and in the year following organized the Consolidated Aircraft Corporation. His firm manufactured many types of airplanes, including the Army's PB-2A fighter and the 0-19 observation plane. In 1928 Consolidated built the XBY-1, a flying boat with a wingspan of 100 feet. This was the first Consolidated flying boat purchased by the United States Navy. Following this came the big thirty-two-place Consolidated *Commodore* flying boat.

The *Commodore* led to the development of the P2Y type of flying boat. This was a two-engined plane with a wingspan of 100 feet and a length of 62 feet. This was the plane which was to lead to the world-famous PBY *Catalina* flying boats. In January, 1934, six P2Y's in the service of the United States Navy made the first successful mass flight from San Francisco to Pearl Harbor, Hawaii, a distance of 2,414 miles.

First introduced in 1934, the Consolidated PBY *Catalina* was one of the world's first all-metal flying boats. Powered with two 600-horsepower radial engines, the PBY was for six years the fastest airplane of its class. In January, 1937, twelve Navy PBY's flew in nonstop formation from San Diego, California, to Pearl Harbor, Hawaii, a distance of 2,553 miles, in 21 hours and 43 minutes. In June of the same year twelve PBY's flew in nonstop formation from San Diego to Coco Solo, Canal Zone, or 3,087 miles in 27 hours and 21 minutes. In 1937 Sir Hubert Wilkins flew a commercial version of the PBY over 19,000 miles of Arctic wastes.

♦ ♦ ♦

30

TECHNICAL PROGRESSIN THE U. S. ARMY AIR CORPS IN THE THIRTIES

Although prevented from any great expansion in the years following World War I, the Army led the way in many phases of aviation. United States Army planes were the first to fly around the world. Army aviation also pioneered night flying and the use of the lighted airfield, refueling in the air, and radio communication between ground and plane. It made great advances in aërial photography. In 1929, Captain Albert W. Stevens photographed Mount Rainier from an airplane 227 miles away, establishing a record of long-distance aërial photography. The same year, Lieutenant "Jimmy" Doolittle, in a demonstration of instrument-flying, accomplished a take-off and a landing solely through the use of instruments. This was the beginning of "blind flying." The Army Fokker *Question Mark* under the command of Carl Spaatz and Ira Eaker, generals commanding our heavy bomber forces in Europe in World War II, established an endurance record by staying aloft for 150 hours. Their plane was refueled in the air during the record flight. Army aviators were trained in the use of oxygen at high altitudes and in the use of instruments for "blind flying."

In 1927 the great Matériel Division of the Air Corps was established in its new home at Wright Field, Dayton, Ohio, close by the birthplace of Orville and Wilbur Wright. The Air Corps Matériel Division was the testing laboratory for all Army aviation equipment. Here all types of new engines, planes, and instruments were developed and tested. Aircraft manufacturers co-operated closely with Army technicians in developing ideas which would help to further the advancement of military aviation. New types of planes were taken to Wright Field, where Army technicians and test pilots put them through grueling tests before releasing them for Army service. Here the Army research engineers worked with oil companies to develop fuels which would increase the performance of aircraft engines. Clothing and equipment for pilots were tested. High-speed aërial cameras were developed, and it was through the efforts of the men at Wright Field that aërial photography in general was perfected to so high a degree.

Many of the features developed for the Army at Wright Field also were applied to commercial aviation and contributed greatly to the safety of air travel. From the earliest postwar days, Army aviation leaders had been insistent that safety was the most important factor in the development of airplanes and of aviation equipment. The experts at Wright Field have contributed greatly to the high record of safety which consistently has prevailed in Army aviation.

THE ALLISON ENGINE

For several years after World War I, all Army airplanes were powered with water-cooled, in-line engines. In the majority of cases it was the *Liberty* engine developed during the war, but some water-cooled Wright engines also were used. As late as 1927 the Army still was experimenting with the *Liberty* engine and trying to increase its horsepower. James A. Allison became interested in this project and, when the job was given up as hopeless, went on to create his own engine. He died before he had completed his engine, but his assistant, Norman H. Gilman, continued its development in conjunction with General Motors. The first successful Allison engine was completed in 1932, and the following year the Navy used it to power the dirigibles *Akron* and *Macon.*

LOCKHEED P-38 *LIGHTNING*

The Army became very much interested in the Allison engine. Although a number of Army fighters were equipped with radials following the early successes of that type of engine, Air Corps men believed that, due to its narrow frontal area, the in-line engine could help to streamline fighters. Finally, in 1939, after many changes, the first Allison engines were installed in Curtiss P-40 Army fighters. The first Allison engine had developed 1,090 horsepower. By 1940 its horsepower was increased to 1,150 and the Army adopted it as standard. It was installed in all P-40's and later in Lawrence Bell's P-39 *Airacobra.* In the P-39 the engine was installed in the fuselage behind the pilot. A ten-foot shaft carried the power to the propeller in the nose of the ship. This installation permitted the housing of a 37-millimeter cannon and two machine guns in the nose of the *Airacobra.* The Lockheed P-38 *Lightning*was powered with two Allison engines, making it the first fighter with more than two thousand horsepower.

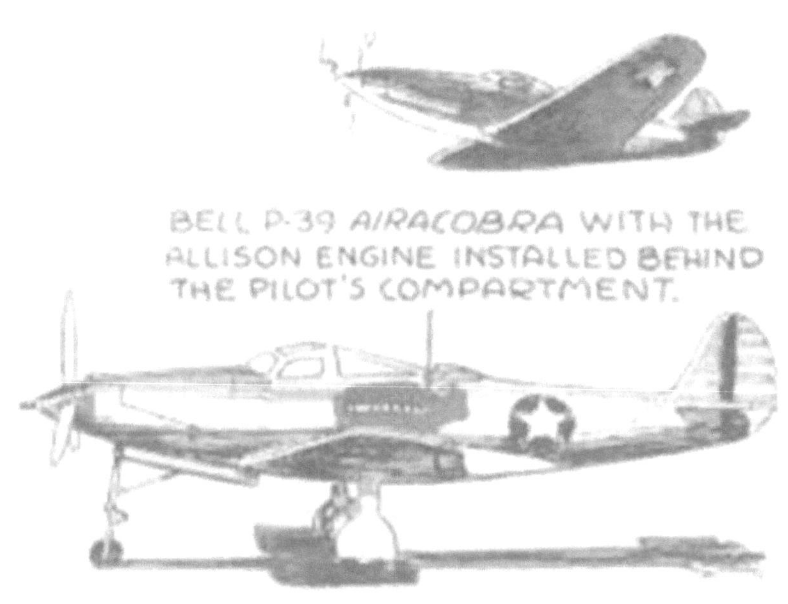

BELL P-39 *AIRACOBRA* WITH THE ALLISON ENGINE INSTALLED BEHIND THE PILOT'S COMPARTMENT.

♦ ♦ ♦

31

BATTLESHIPS OFTHE AIRLEAD THE WAY TO VICTORY

Regardless of the fact that this country was at peace and our military policy a defensive one, our farseeing Air Corps leaders continued to build American air power around the heavy, long-range bomber. As the heavy bomber was primarily an offensive weapon, many Americans believed the Army's development of it to be contrary to our declared policy. As a result, we did not build great numbers of bombers. However, with the small number that we did have, our Army aviators made great progress in the technique of high-altitude bombing.

As in all branches of the United States Army, great stress was laid on good marksmanship. Army aviators were trained to hit the mark with their bombs just as the infantryman does with his rifle. Other countries developing heavy bombers were satisfied if their airmen dropped a great many bombs in a given target area. In this country the development of the bombsight enabled our aviators to hit a target with great accuracy from high altitudes. This is called precision bombing. It was also known as pin-pointing a target, because of the ability of our bombardiers to score direct hits on small targets. It was the B-17 *Flying Fortress* that gave Army airmen the greatest help in perfecting high-altitude, precision bombing. The broad wings of the *Fortress* furnished a steady platform from which to aim the bombs, and the great plane was able to fly smoothly in the higher altitudes. The bombardier riding in its transparent nose could carefully line up his target and drop his bombs with precision accuracy.

It was not until the outbreak of World War II that most Americans came to realize the value of the airplane in modern conflict. As the fighting grew to global proportions, Americans began in particular to appreciate the farsightedness of our Air Corps leaders in developing the long-range bomber.

By 1940 the original Boeing 299 or B-17 had grown from a sixteen-ton ship to a giant twenty-two-ton bomber. The new version, the B-17D, was powered with two 1,200-horsepower radial engines, giving it a speed of more than 300 miles per hour. Continual improvements were made on it and by the spring of 1942 a still more formidable member of the *Fortress* family, the B-17F, was in production.

The B-17F was the most powerful bomber yet produced. It was armed with eleven .50-caliber machine guns and manned by a crew of ten. It could carry more than three tons of bombs to targets over seven hundred miles distant. Its oxygen system permitted its crew to fly the *Fortress* at altitudes above 35,000 feet. With its eleven heavy machine guns in the hands of a perfectly trained crew, the *Fortress* was capable of defending itself with deadly effectiveness.

The first *Flying Fortresses* went into action with the United States Army on the day after the attack on Pearl Harbor. Although this country had then only a limited number of *Fortresses*, they and their successors quickly began to distinguish themselves on the battlefronts of the world.

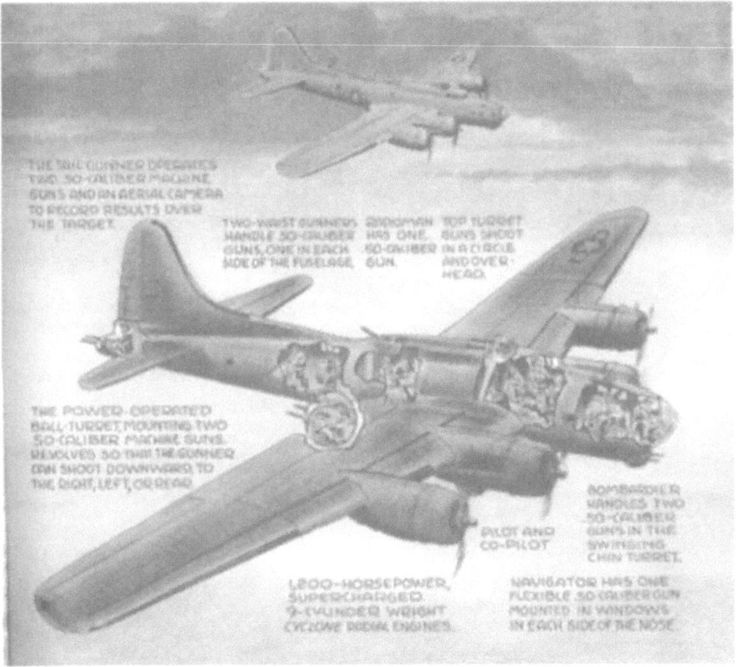

By the summer of 1942 *Flying Fortresses* had begun what was to be the greatest sustained aërial invasion the world had ever known. Starting with a small group of *Fortresses*, the United States Army Air Forces went to work to wreck Adolf Hitler's "Fortress Europe" and clear the path for an Allied invasion.

From small raids by a dozen *Fortresses* the number of bombers grew until the raids became huge aërial invasions involving hundreds of bombers and thousands of airmen. That the path for invasion was cleared and victory brought nearer was due in no small measure to our big bombers and the farsighted American airmen who had brought them into being against almost insurmountable obstacles.

♦ ♦ ♦

32

ARMY ATTACK AVIATIONAND TRAINING

Although the airplane in World War I had been used mainly as an observation and a plane-to-plane combat weapon, wise American airmen, such as General "Billy" Mitchell, visualized the craft as a means of destroying the enemy's ability to fight. These men saw his weapons destroyed as they were being built and his transport stopped before it reached the battlefield. As the result of this thinking, our doctrine of air power was established.

With this much accomplished, the need for various types of airplanes was clearly defined. It called for three distinct types of warplanes: the long-range bomber, the observation plane, and the pursuit plane. Air strategy was built around the long-range bomber. This was the weapon which would destroy the enemy's war plants and military establishments on his home grounds. The observation plane was to be used to seek out the enemy's movements and to locate his installations. As aërial photography was perfected, the observation planes were to be equipped to bring back a record of their findings. These records would establish the targets for the long-range bombers. In the beginning, the pursuit plane was considered a weapon to protect our own military establishments, our cities, and our war plants. Its mission was to intercept any enemy planes attempting to attack us.

On the preceding pages we have seen the bomber develop from a single-engined DH-4 into the giant four-engined B-17. This development was the result of the careful study of aërial strategy by our Army airmen. When the big bombers with a range of thousands of miles were built, our strategists saw them as weapons to be used only against an enemy's most distant military establishments. The smaller two-engined bombers which had once been our long-range bomberswere delegated to the destruction of targets closer to the battlefronts.

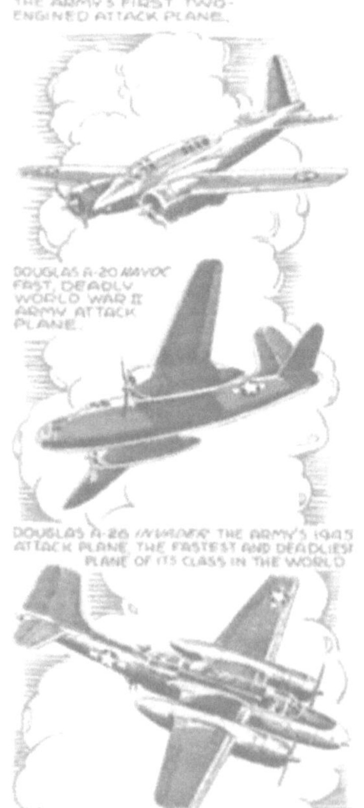

In time, the use of the two-engine bomber led to the development of attack aviation. This was built around very fast, two-engined planes which could carry both bombs and guns. These medium bombers were to be used to attack targets of medium range with both bombs and guns. They were to be used to destroy enemy troops, transports, and gun emplacements. In the few years of World War II, attack bombers were developed from comparatively slow planes to ships with the speed of fighters. They are capable of carrying more than a ton of bombs, and of mounting cannon and as many as fifteen machine guns.

With the establishment of a definite policy of air strategy, plans were worked out for the training of personnel to man and service our fighting planes. The training plans set up in the early twenties are essentially the same as those in effect at the present. The system consisted of two training schools, Primary and Advanced. In the Primary School cadets received their preliminary flight training and studied construction of planes, radio, weather observation, and other technical problems concerning flight. The qualities shown by the cadets in the primary training helped to determine the branch of combat aviation for which they were best fitted.

At the Advanced School, cadets were trained in larger and more powerful airplanes and received instruction in gunnery, formation flying, cross-country flying, and night flying. Graduates of the Advanced School received their wings and, by joining tactical units, completed their training as members of regular service squadrons. In 1928 all Army air training activities were consolidated at one great training center at San Antonio, Texas. This great headquarters for the training of United States Army airmen was dedicated in June, 1930, as Randolph Field, in memory of Captain William M. Randolph. Captain Randolph, a native of Texas, had lost his life in an airplane crash a few years before. It was fitting that the first great Army aviation training program was under the direction of Brigadier General Frank P. Lahm, the Army's pioneer aviator.

♦ ♦ ♦

33

SUPER-FIGHTER

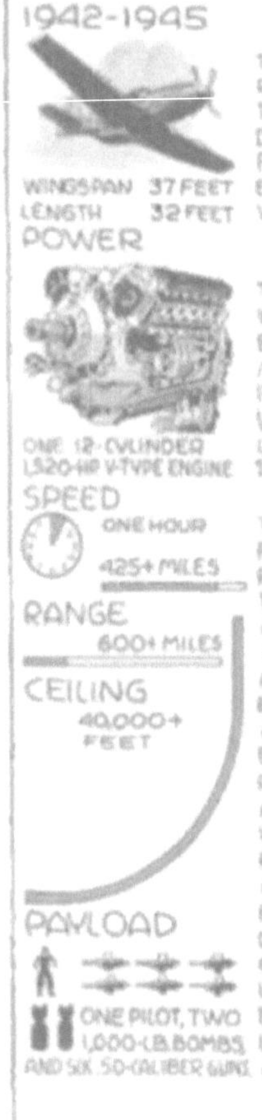

In the Pacific American fighters dropped down from 25,000 feet, screamed across an enemy airfield, guns blasting, and indicators showing a speed of over eight miles a minute. If the Japanese had not been "dug in," they probably would have been sucked into the planes' airscoops. Later one of the pilots expressed the sentiments of the entire raiding group when he said, "It's a wonderful feeling to watch that air speed indicator climb. It makes you feel that nothing on this earth can catch you."

That pilot was talking about the North American P-51 *Mustang*. He was not exaggerating when he made his remark, for there has been no fighter in action that could equal its speed. In the *Mustang* we see streamlining at its best. Its in-line, liquid-cooled engine offers only a very small frontal area and allows the *Mustang* to have the narrow fuselage of the fastest racing plane. This narrow fuselage and the high-speed wing practically eliminate all drag that reduces speed. The landing gear retracts completely into the fuselage and also eliminates drag. Even the air scoop is placed far back under the fuselage where it offers practically no resistance. The reduction of drag to a minimum eliminates vibration to such an extent that the pilot of a *Mustang* flies at terrific speeds with no ill effects.

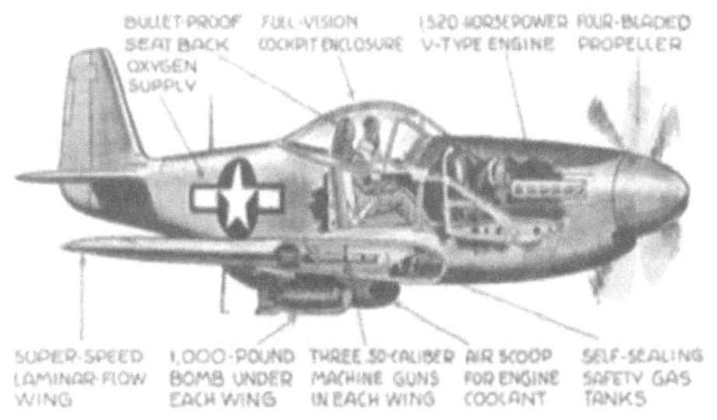

The *Mustang* was designed and built as the result of a careful study of modern fighter tactics. It grew out of the need for high-speed, high-altitude fighters to serve as escorts for our heavy bombers. As our bomber attacks against Germany grew in strength, the Nazis in desperation threw in hundreds of their fighters to hinder us. The *Mustang*, with its tremendous speed and ability to fight at high altitudes, proved a sensation as an escort fighter. Two *Mustang* groups alone have accounted for the destruction of almost two thousand Nazi fighters. With a speed of over 425 miles per hour and capable of great range, *Mustangs* spelled doom to Nazi air power.

♦ ♦ ♦

MAN-MADE THUNDERBOLTS RIP WIDE A PATH TO VICTORY

The Republic P-4-7 *Thunderbolt* was planned in 1940 as the result of the Air Corps' desire to strengthen our fighter squadrons. A study of the Nazis' use of crushing air power in their attacks on Western Europe hastened our plans to build heavier and more powerful fighters.

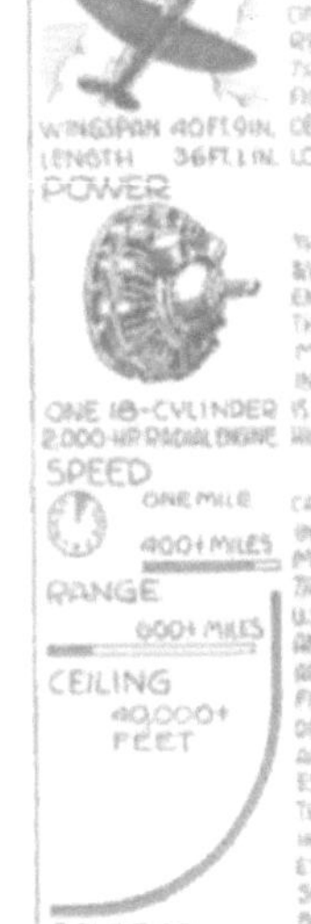

At one of the Air Corps meetings with aircraft manufacturers at Wright Field in 1940, Alexander Kartveli sketched on the back of an envelope an idea for a super-fighter. Eight months later his idea had grown into the fastest and most powerful fighter ever built in this country.

Alexander Kartveli was chief engineer for Republic Aviation Corporation. His sketches were developed by his firm to produce the six-and-one-half-ton, 400-mile-an-hour P-47 fighter. The P-47 was the answer to the Army's demands for a big, powerfully armed fighter which could out-fly and out-fight any warplane put into the skies by an enemy. More than 10,000 *Thunderbolts* have been built since 1940 and they have taken a terrific toll of Axis planes, both in Europe and in the Pacific. Pilots of one group of *Thunderbolts* that operated in the Pacific shot down Jap planes at the rate of 52 to 1.

The Republic P-47 *Thunderbolt* proved to be one of the most versatile airplanes developed in this war. It performs equally well at high or low altitudes. Armed with eight .50-caliber machine guns, it is a hard-hitting escort fighter which can out-fight any plane sent up to hinder our big bombers. When used for ground strafing it has no superior. With two

1000-pound bombs tucked under its wings it becomes a deadly dive-bomber. Armed with rocket tubes and its eight big machine guns blazing, it can blast enemy tanks, transport, and gun emplacements effectively.

♦ ♦ ♦

35

SUPERFORTRESS

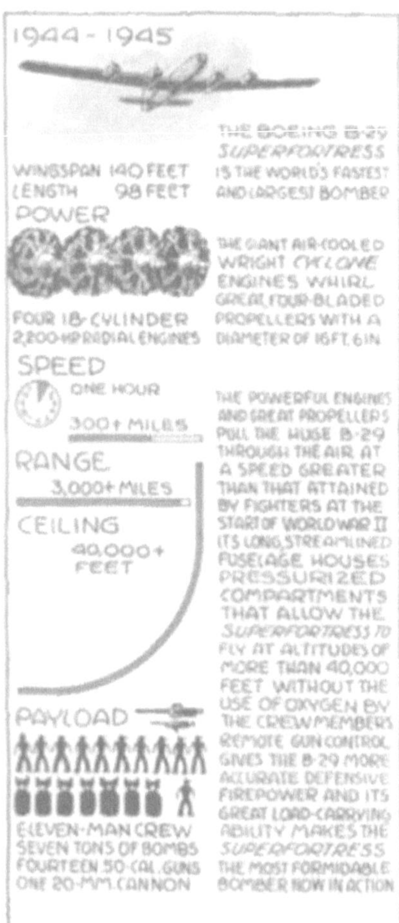

The first giant *Flying Fortress* had hardly taken off from the Boeing factory at Seattle, in 1935, before its engineers began to think about bigger and faster super-bombers. As the new *Fortresses* shattered records for speed, pay load, distance, and altitude, farsighted Air Corps leaders also began to think about more powerful super-bombers.

By 1937 the brains and labor of Boeing engineers and production men created the first of the super-bombers. It was the giant Boeing XB-15 and it actually dwarfed the *Flying Fortress.* With a gross weight of 35 tons, 13 tons more than the *Fortress,* the XB-15 was 20 feet longer, 3 feet higher, and had a wingspan 45 feet greater. Its general appearance, however, was patterned after the *Fortress.* Only one XB-15 was built. It was used for experimental purposes by the Air Corps, and the Boeing Company went ahead to build the high-altitude *Stratoliner* and the big *Clipper* planes for civilian use.

Thus it was that even before the Nazis swept into Poland in 1939 the Air Corps had been thinking of an airplane that would dwarf the *Flying Fortress.* Size alone was not enough. General Arnold and his associates wanted an airplane which would carry a heavier bomb load farther, faster, and higher than ever before.

Few people aside from the Army knew of the XB-15, and the development of the super-bomber was one of the best kept secrets in history. One of the greatest surprises of the war was the War Department's announcement on June 15, 1944: "B-29 *Superfortresses* of the United States Army Air Forces' 20th Bomber Command bombed Japan."

Just one year after the announcement of the first *Superfortress* attack on Japan, five hundred of these giant ships took part in a single raid against targets on the Japanese mainland. In groups of four and five hundred they blasted Japan almost daily. *Superfortresses* bombed Japan to her knees in the spring and summer of 1945. Then in August of that year a lone *Superfortress* dropped the world's first atomic bomb on Hiroshima for the knockout blow that brought us victory.

Half again as large as the *Flying Fortress*, the *Superfortress* carries twice the load of the *Fortress*. It has a wingspan of 141 feet and its highly streamlined fuselage is 98 feet long. Powered with the largest engines yet in service, it has a speed far in excess of 300 miles per hour. The pressurized cabin of the B-29 permits its crew to fly without the use of heated suits or oxygen masks at substratosphere altitudes. In military terms this means better physical condition, more skilful gunnery, more accurate bombing, and more comfort for the crews. In the *Superfortress* we see great ideas, born years ago in the minds of our airmen, come into being with overwhelming and disastrous effects on our enemies throughout the Pacific.

♦ ♦ ♦

36

NAVAL AVIATION IN THE EARLY MONTHS OF WORLD WAR II

Just as the United States was approaching the brink of war, the Navy air arm owned only about a thousand airplanes of all types. The young Navy airmen who had perfected dive-bombing had seen their invention adopted by the Nazis and used with deadly effect in their march across Western Europe. In the year before Pearl Harbor the Navy had acquired only a few hundred new airplanes. We did have, however, a group of young men who had been living and breathing aviation for the past fifteen years. They knew what was needed in the way of new fighting planes and they knew how to train thousands of new naval aviators when the time came. But it took the tremendous sweeps of the Nazis in Europe and the shadow of Japan across the Pacific to unloose the flood of fighting planes which was to give the United States Navy the greatest aërial fighting force ever launched.

At the time of the attack on Pearl Harbor we had seven carriers, including our first big ones, the *Lexington* and the *Saratoga.* The Grumman F4F *Wildcat* was our standard carrier-based fighter. We had a small number of TBD *Devastator* torpedo planes and SDB *Dauntless* dive-bombers. Our battleships and cruisers were equipped with Vought OS2U *Kingfisher* and Curtis SO3C *Seagull* observation scout planes launched from the ships' catapults. The Navy was fairly well equipped with PBY *Catalina* long-range patrol bombers. But in the engineering offices of aircraft manufacturers, new and more powerful fighters, bombers, and patrol planes were being planned.

When Japan struck we had eleven aircraft carriers under construction, and two thousand new planes went into service for the Navy. Great training stations were being put into service to increase the Navy's flying personnel to over 15,000 men.

A new patrol bomber, the long-range Martin PBM-1 *Mariner*, went into service for the Navy in 1941. It had a wingspan of 118 feet and a length of 77 feet 2 inches. It was powerfully armed and carried a heavy load of bombs. It was capable of long range and was able to carry out extensive over-ocean patrols without returning to its base. Ample living accommodations were provided for its eleven-man crew. In addition to its duties as an anti-submarine patrol and long-range bomber, the *Mariner* was used as a Navy transport.

The Vought F4U-1 *Corsair* fighters began to go into service in the Pacific soon after the attack on Pearl Harbor. The *Corsair* was a single-place fighter of unusual design. Its wing had the shape of an inverted gull wing. This design allowed clearance for the *Corsair's* 13-foot, 4-inch propeller. A straight wing would have needed a dangerously high landing gear to provide clearance for such a large propeller. Originally designed for carrier use, the 2,000-horsepower, 400-mile-an-hour *Corsair* was adopted for land-based operations by the United States Marine Corps. Marine Corps aviators used the *Corsair* with deadly effect against the Japs from Guadalcanal on. Navy pilots flew the *Corsair* as a night-fighter to put a stop to the Jap's habit of bombing our Pacific airfields at night.

The Navy's newest torpedo plane, the Grumman TBF *Avenger*, first appeared in the battle off Midway. The big *Avenger* had a speed of 270 miles per hour, a range of 1,400 miles, and carried a 2,000-pound bomb load or a full-sized torpedo concealed in its fuselage. The famous Torpedo Squadron 8, in fourteen weeks sank as many Jap warships including two aircraft carriers and one battleship; bombed one heavy cruiser, one light cruiser, and a number of smaller ships.

Avengers helped to pave the way for the establishment of bases in the Pacific. *Corsairs*, used as the Navy's first night-fighters, broke up Japanese night bombings of the newly won island bases and allowed our hard-worked men to rest at night.

♦ ♦ ♦

37

THE U. S. NAVY'S DEADLIEST FIGHTER PLANE

In the months following Pearl Harbor the tough little Grumman F4F *Wildcat* was ever in the thick of the fight in the Pacific. Based on the few carriers available for use against the Japs, the *Wildcats* outfought overwhelming numbers of enemy warplanes. Over the Marshall Islands in February, 1942, *Wildcat* fighters bagged ten Jap fighters and three bombers without any American losses. At Wake Island, a lone *Wildcat*, manned by a Marine, bombed a Jap cruiser to the bottom. Lieutenant Commander Edward ("Butch") O'Hare was flying a *Wildcat* when he brought down six Jap bombers singlehanded in a few minutes. Such incidents were typical of *Wildcat* action in the first year of the war.

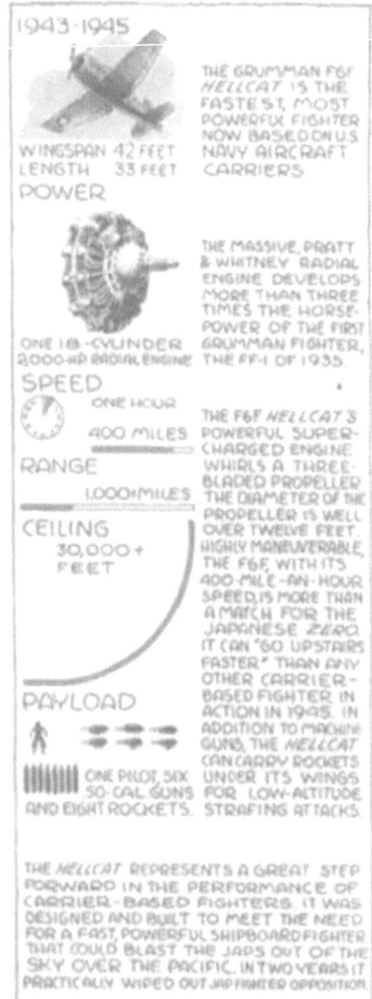

When President Roosevelt presented the Congressional Medal of Honor to "Butch" O'Hare, he asked him what kind of fighter was needed to beat the Japs. O'Hare replied, "Something that will go upstairs faster." Commander John Thatch, master Navy combat technician, had told Grumman officials the same thing, and had added a request for more speed in general. Not many months later, the roar of a 2,000-horsepower echoed over Long Island, New York, and a new Grumman fighter began to "go upstairs faster."

The new fighter that answered the Navy pilots' demand for more speed and more power was the Grumman F6F *Hellcat.* Much larger than its baby brother the *Wildcat*, the *Hellcat* was powered with an eighteen-cylinder Pratt & Whitney radial engine. The big radial developed over 2,000 horsepower and put the *Hellcat* in the 400-mile-an-hour class. It proved to be one of the most maneuverable fighters in the world and could climb like a skyrocket. The cockpit housed atop the big fuselage at its highest point gave pilots excellent visibility to train the *Hellcat's* six .50-caliber guns on the enemy.

The *Hellcat* has plenty of protective armor for its pilot. It has rubber gasoline tanks encased in canvas hammocks giving them great flexibility in resisting the penetration of bullets and shell fragments. The *Hellcat* handles beautifully at all altitudes. At high altitudes it could more than outfight any plane that the Japs sent up. It is also a deadly weapon when used in low-altitude strafing attacks against airfields and shipping. The

Hellcat has now replaced the *Wildcat* as the standard fighter based on our aircraft carriers. Much of our success in driving the Japs out of the air over the Pacific is due to the *Hellcat.* These powerful fighters, based on the carriers of Admiral Halsey's famous Task Force 58, carried their devastating attacks to the Japs' homeland.

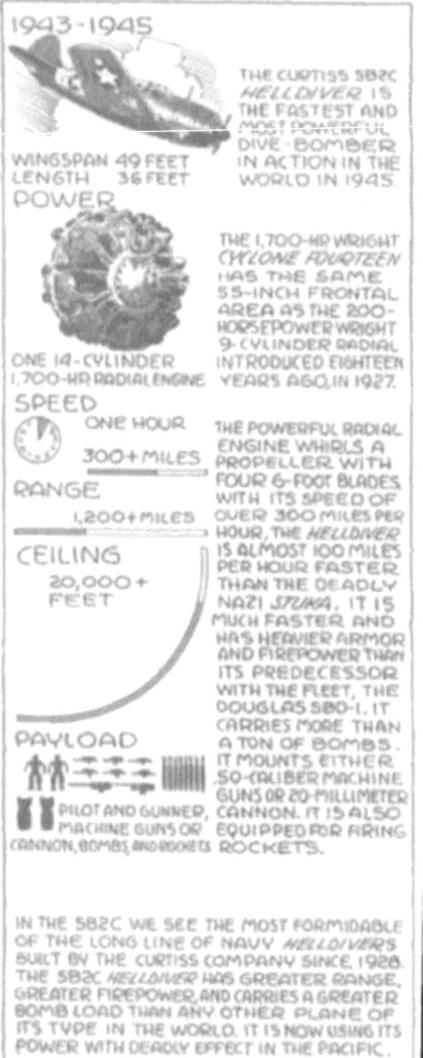

Although dive-bombing was originated by Navy airmen it was a number of years before an airplane was built that was rugged enough to stand up under the shock of repeated dives. The first airplane built specifically for dive-bombing was a Curtiss F8C *Helldiver*, built in 1929. This original dive-bomber was a biplane. The series continued until 1935 when Curtiss introduced the SBC type of dive-bomber. This was also a biplane with wire bracing. The streamlining in the SBC was much improved and it was equipped with a retractable landing gear. The SBC was also called the *Helldiver.* While the SBC series marked advance in dive-bomber performance, the biplane wings and wire bracing created a drag which held down its diving speed. In 1939 the Curtiss Company began to work on a new dive-bomber design.

In the meantime Douglas had brought out the all-metal, low-wing SBD *Dauntless* dive-bomber. This was a fast, clean airplane equipped with flaps for diving. The flaps, attached to the trailing edge of the wing, could be dropped down to act as brakes. The flaps created a resistance which cut the speed of the plane at the will of the pilot. Powered with a 1,000-horsepower radial engine, the SBD had a speed of about 200 miles per hour. It carried a 1,000-pound bomb under its fuselage which, when released by the pilot, was swung clear of the plane by a yokelike gear. The SBD usually started its dive at an altitude of 10,000 feet. From that height the plane could pick up a speed of from 450 to 500 miles per hour. The best speed for dive-bombing is about 275 miles per hour, and the flaps on the SBD enabled the pilot to control his speed as he dived on his target.

At the time of the Japanese attack on Pearl Harbor, the SBD was the standard dive-bomber based on our carriers. From the very start it was a star performer in our war in the Pacific. In the first years of the struggle SBD's destroyed more enemy planes, ships, and property than did all our other air and surface weapons combined. SBD's were in the forefront in our war in the Pacific. But a giant new dive-bomber suddenly appeared over Rabaul, New Guinea, in the fall of 1944, the deadliest bomber which had yet dived on the Japs. Another *Helldiver* was in action.

♦ ♦ ♦

38

DIVE-BOMBER

This big dive-bomber was the one begun by Curtiss in 1939. Few planes in history had been so long in the development stage, but when the SB2C *Helldiver* did appear it was the biggest and fastest dive-bomber to go into service with the United States Navy. Powered with a 1,700-horsepower, 14-cylinder, Wright Cyclone radial engine, its top speed is in excess of 300 miles per hour. Carrying more than a ton of bombs, it has a range of over 1,200 miles. It is armed with either .50-caliber machine guns or 20-millimeter cannon. It is also equipped to carry rockets under its wings.

♦ ♦ ♦

39

OUR FLYING NAVY

From Pearl Harbor, Guadalcanal, and Midway to Tokyo Bay Our Gallant Navy Men, Carriers, and Planes Led the Way to Victory and Have Added Many Heroic Chapters to the Glorious History of the United States Navy.

When the Japs struck at Pearl Harbor on Sunday morning December 7, 1941, United States naval aviation had just passed its thirtieth birthday. At no time in its history had the U. S. Navy been confronted with a greater task. Many of our great warships lay in the mud at Pearl Harbor. Many of our Navy planes had been destroyed, and Japan controlled the greater part of the western Pacific.

Though the future looked black, our Navy possessed one great asset, invisible to most of us. It was that small group of Navy airmen who had lived and breathed flying since our first carriers were launched. So thorough had been the schooling and the thinking of our pioneer flat-top men that, when war did come, they were ready. These naval aviators who had created and tested every form of air tactics were ready to put them into action. They also were able to pass on their lessons to the large group of young men who were to man the thousands of warplanes being built for the Navy.

As the new planes were rolling off the production lines and the new naval aviators were in training, the old-timers went to work on the Japs in the Pacific. That they did their job well is testified by the fact that the Japs did not get back to Pearl Harbor or attack our west coast. With only a few carriers to cover the vast Pacific area, and a pitifully small number of airplanes, our naval aviators carried the fight all the way down to the Solomons. They helped take and hold Guadalcanal. They stopped the great Japanese fleet at Midway and drove them out of the Aleutians. Navy flat-tops took "Jimmy" Doolittle and his Tokyo raiders almost to Japan's front door. Wherever our naval aviators met the enemy they knocked him out of the air at the rate of five to one.

In spite of our favorable ratio of victories over the Japs in the air, they still outnumbered us ten to one in the Pacific. During 1942 many new Navy airplanes were delivered. Thousands of young naval aviators were trained at our naval air stations. A great naval air transport service was created to fly men and materials to distant Pacific islands. With only one carrier, the *Enterprise*, left in the Pacific, a great new carrier fleet was rushed into service.

By the Fall of 1943 a tremendous change was wrought in the Pacific. In September the first three new carriers, the *Essex*, the *Yorktown*, and the *Independence*, were battle-tested in the raid on Marcus Island. *Avengers* and *Hellcats* began to appear in great numbers to take the place of *Wildcats* on the decks of our big carriers. Raid followed raid. The Gilbert Island chain, Tarawa, Kwajalein, Truk, Palau, Saipan, and other islands fell before the blows of our new carrier-based air power.

More big new carriers continued to appear in the Pacific and a new type of sea power came into being, the carrier task force. Here we saw air power based on a great fleet of large and small carriers forming the spearhead of a naval offensive. The flat-top had truly become the "Queen of the Fleet."

Now we see come into being the ideas born in the minds of a group of pioneer naval aviators twenty years ago. The airplane has not only gone to sea with the fleet but, as the striking power of the Navy, it is leading the fleet to victory.

It was the work of the fighting planes based on Admiral Marc A. Mitscher's carrier Task Force 58 that hammered a path to the very front door of Japan.

Since Pearl Harbor, naval aviators have shot down over ten thousand Japanese aircraft with the loss of less than two thousand of our own planes. This gives our Navy pilots a score of better than five to one. These figures include the dark days of the first year of war when our Navy boys were outnumbered ten to one.

From a force of a few carriers and a handful of moderately fast warplanes, naval aviation grew, in three years, to the world's greatest sea-borne air force. The speed of our fighters increased by more than a hundred miles an hour. Our dive-bombers and torpedo planes, the world's finest, tripled their bomb and torpedo loads. Our big patrol bombers and transports fly the Pacific unarmed.

Jack Towers, who in 1911 was one of the Navy's first three aviators, is now Vice Admiral Towers, Air Chief of the Pacific. John Pride, one of the first aviators to fly from the deck of the *Langley*, is now a rear admiral with our Pacific aërial task forces. Pioneers of naval aviation such as Admirals Ballentine, Sherman, Clark, Radford, and others are all in the

Pacific. These men, none of them much over fifty years old, are practical flying officers. Many of the other men, who for the past twenty years or more have devoted themselves to the development of naval aviation, are also rear admirals. That is fitting, for it was they who kept naval aviation alive in the days of peace.

♦ ♦ ♦

40

AËRIAL ARMADA

From a Mere Handful of Men and Machines in 1940 the U. S. Army Air Forces Grew Into the Greatest Aërial Task Force That the World Has Ever Known. That Air Force Shortened the War by Years and Helped to Bring Us Total Victory in 1945.

As in World War I, we have seen Army aviation reach the brink of war without being fully prepared. Again we have seen our military leaders and aircraft builders roll up their sleeves and go to work. However, we have never seen anything to equal the development of our Army Air Forces.

From a force which numbered hardly more than 100,000 men and a handful of airplanes at the time of the attack on Pearl Harbor, the United States Army Air Forces have grown to be the world's greatest aërial striking power. On December 7, 1941, Army aviation had 3,000 combat planes, only 1,157 of which were actually fit for first-line duty. In all United States territory we had only 159 four-engined bombers. The Curtiss P-40 was our only fighter in production in any quantity.

Less than three years after Pearl Harbor the Army Air Forces could send out 1,000 four-engined bombers on a single raid. Eight or nine hundred fighters could accompany them as escorts. More than 200,000 warplanes have been built in this country since Pearl Harbor, and the Air Forces can boast of thousands of planes instead of hundreds of them. Army Air Forces' bases are in operation over the entire globe.

Complete airfields have been carved out of jungle and Arctic wastes. These airfields are equipped to keep our warplanes in perfect repair without the loss of time from combat duty. To build and equip these fields, millions of tons of materials have been transported thousands of miles. More than two million men have been trained to fly our planes and to keep them flying. Our great training system took thousands of green young men from civilian life and trained them in the several hundred skills necessary to keep our planes in safe fighting trim. Air Forces men work in every sort of climate, from the frozen north to the steaming jungles of the

South Pacific. The Air Forces experts at Wright Field developed clothing, materials, and equipment to keep our planes in flying and fighting condition regardless of climate or weather. The training, equipping, and development of personnel and matériel for the giant United States Army Air Forces is truly a modern miracle.

Between the years 1943-1945 we saw our air strategy, planned years ago, put into deadly effect under the leadership of the men who originated it. Only General "Billy" Mitchell failed to live to see his ideas at work in defeating the Nazis and the Japs. The United States Army Air Forces today represents American air power, just as he prophesied many years ago.

The very best proof of the splendid development of Army aviation is the box score built up by World War II aviators against our enemies. From December 7, 1941, to January 1, 1945, they destroyed 29,316 enemy aircraft and dropped 1,220,000 tons of bombs on enemy territory. Our losses in this period were but 13,491 planes. This, it should be remembered, was against enemies who had been preparing for years with the purpose of defeating us.

When the Japanese attacked Pearl Harbor, the commercial airlines of the United States were operating 341 transport planes. Almost at once the Army and Navy began to take over transport planes from the airlines for war service. The Army organized the Air Transport Command. This new branch of the Air Forces, under the command of Major General Harold L. George, a former Air Plans officer, started in the Spring of 1942 in a one-room office with a personnel of three men. Since that time the Air Transport Command has grown to be the world's largest airline. In addition to operating Army transport planes, the Air Transport Command contracted with the country's major airlines to fly Army men and materials. Thus many of the transport planes which in peacetime flew over our countryside went into war service and began to fly over distant lands. All the major airlines contributed planes and crews to the vital needs of war. DC-3's, which a few weeks before had been flying between our big cities, began to fly over oceans and mountain ranges in every quarter of the globe. At the start most of the planes used for Air Transport Command cargo were Douglas DC-3's and DC-2's and a few Boeing *Stratoliners*. The new Douglas DC-4's being built for the airlines when war began went right off the production lines into service for the Army or Navy. The Navy also developed their own air transport service and operated in a manner similar to the ATC. This group was known as the Naval Air Transport Service or NATS. The Army Air Transport Command operated its own weather stations, radio ranges, and airfields in the same manner as the commercial lines did in peacetime. Planes flew vital war cargo and personnel on systematic airline procedure. Millions of miles were flown daily by planes rushing tons of men and materials to the far-flung battlefronts of the world. Practically every bit of matériel taken into China during the first three years of war was flown in over some of the worst flying terrain in the world. The work of the Air Transport Command, the Naval Air Transport Service, and the major airlines has been one of the truly magnificent jobs of the war. Pan American's first transatlantic competitor, American Export Airlines, started its first service in 1942 flying wartime cargo.

The research and safety devices developed in peacetime by our commercial airlines played a tremendous part in the success of our world-wide wartime transport service. Not only did the airlines furnish planes and crews for the war effort, but they also set up schools and trained hundreds of transport pilots, crews, ground service men, and operations men for the military transport service.

The experience gained in operating such a great global air transport system has not only helped materially to win the war, but will be invaluable in expanding peacetime air transport and cargo service. New methods of handling cargo of all weights during the war will speed the development of postwar air cargo service. The world-wide experience of the transport crews will be valuable in developing postwar air travel to distant lands. Hundreds of new air crews trained for war service will be available for the great expansion of commercial aviation in early postwar days.

NORTHROP P-61 *BLACK WIDOW*
NIGHT FIGHTER

Forty-two years after the birth of the airplane, we see aviation on the threshold of a great new era of progress. Fighting planes with a speed of nine miles a minute are an actuality. A giant transport plane, capable of carrying 100 passengers, has flown across the continent in six hours. This means that a passenger may eat lunch in New York and dinner in California. It means that postwar air travelers will become accustomed to flying at the speed of our 1939 fighting planes. Air travelers soon will be crossing the country at a speed of eight miles a minute. Boys and girls reading this book will, a few years from now, marvel that we even got excited over the eight-mile-a-minute airplane.

The year 1944 saw a twelve-and-one-half ton fighter go into action on the war fronts. This plane, the Northrop P-61 *Black Widow* night-fighter, is one of the most powerful airplanes yet to go into action. Powered with two 2,000-horsepower engines, the P-61 flies at 400 miles per hour. Equipped with radar and powerful guns, it can search out an enemy plane at night and destroy it.

The new Bell P-59 *Airacomet* is America's first jet-propelled fighter. Its performance has amazed expert test pilots. It has no propeller (note diagram below), and the pilot hears no engine roar or propeller scream. He feels no vibration. Yet he whizzes along at a tremendous speed which is still a military secret. This lack of vibration reduces pilot fatigue, adding hours to his safe flying time.

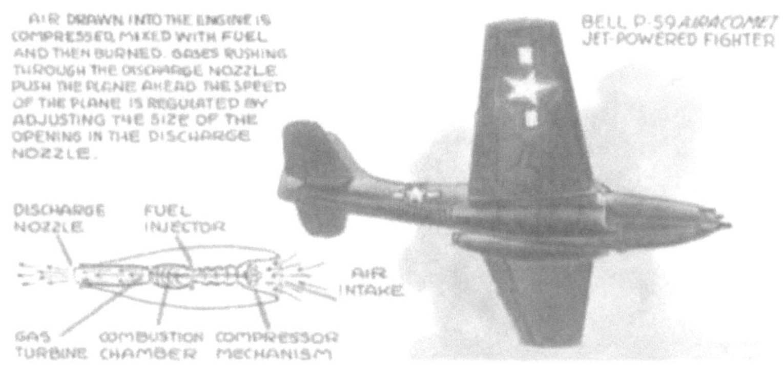

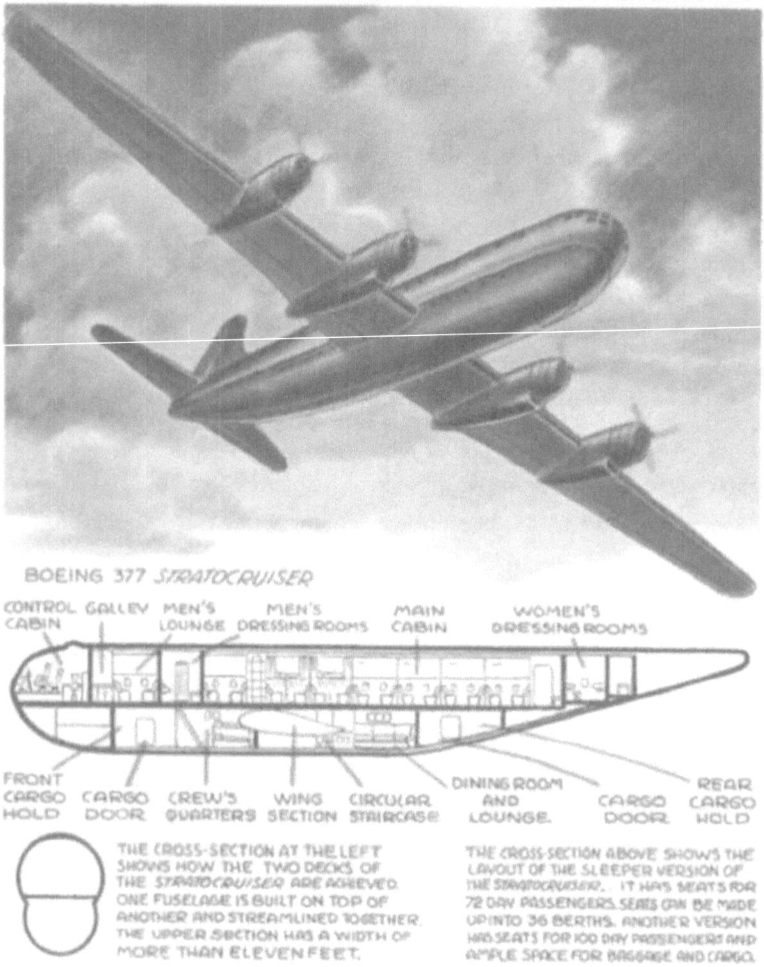

BOEING 377 *STRATOCRUISER*

CONTROL CABIN
GALLEY
MEN'S LOUNGE
MEN'S DRESSING ROOMS
MAIN CABIN
WOMEN'S DRESSING ROOMS
FRONT CARGO HOLD
CARGO DOOR
CREW'S QUARTERS
WING SECTION
CIRCULAR STAIRCASE
DINING ROOM AND LOUNGE
CARGO DOOR
REAR CARGO HOLD

THE CROSS-SECTION AT THE LEFT SHOWS HOW THE TWO DECKS OF THE *STRATOCRUISER* ARE ACHIEVED. ONE FUSELAGE IS BUILT ON TOP OF ANOTHER AND STREAMLINED TOGETHER. THE UPPER SECTION HAS A WIDTH OF MORE THAN ELEVEN FEET.

THE CROSS-SECTION ABOVE SHOWS THE LAYOUT OF THE SLEEPER VERSION OF THE *STRATOCRUISER*. IT HAS SEATS FOR 72 DAY PASSENGERS. SEATS CAN BE MADE UP INTO 36 BERTHS. ANOTHER VERSION HAS SEATS FOR 100 DAY PASSENGERS AND AMPLE SPACE FOR BAGGAGE AND CARGO.

SIKORSKY HELICOPTER

41

POSTWAR AVIATION

In the high-flying, high-speed *Stratocruiser* and the fast *Liberator Liner* we see a type of transport that will become familiar in early postwar days. The development of airplanes with great load-carrying ability will have a great effect on the cost of air travel. Transports like the 100-passenger *Stratocruiser* will soon bring the cost of air travel within the reach of anyone who now can afford regular train fares.

Postwar days will also see a great increase in the use of air cargo planes. Typical of the cargo plane of the future is the Fairchild C-82 *Packet*, now in use as a military transport. The big, roomy cabin of the *Packet* is only slightly smaller than a standard railroad boxcar. As an Army transport, the *Packet* can carry forty-two fully equipped paratroopers or seventy regular troops. As a hospital plane, it has space for thirty-four litter cases and four attendants or seventy-five walking casualties. When used for cargo movement the *Packet's* stern door opens to take a load of jeeps, trucks, artillery, munitions, and other military cargo equal in weight to nine tons. It is readily seen how valuable the *Packet* will be in postwar days. With its range of 3,500 miles, it will speed commercial cargo across the country at reasonable costs. In fact, all the big transports, such as the

Stratocruiser or the *Liberator Liner*, are designed so that they may be converted to all-cargo planes. In the near future perishable foods and other merchandise, which heretofore have taken several days to cross the country, will make the trip overnight.

With the coming of peace, air transport and commercial aviation will grow by leaps and bounds. All the leading airlines and many new ones are planning expanded schedules and looking forward to a great boom in air travel. New transport planes are going into production in the plants of all America's well-known aircraft manufacturers. The new airliners will not only be much faster, but they will also be equipped with every device that will make the air traveler more comfortable. The new airliners will be so fast that there will be no need for sleeper planes on coast-to-coast trips. Sleeper planes will be used only on long overseas trips. The planes will all carry more passengers during the day and that means that air travel will be almost as economical as surface travel.

The big planes for world travel will be ships like the seventy-ton *Martin Mars* flying boat and the giant Pan American Consolidated 204-passenger Model 37. Donald Douglas is building two new luxury airliners, the fifty-passenger DC-6 and the 108-passenger DC-7. The 100-passenger Lockheed *Constellation* will also be in service soon. Smaller planes operating on feeder lines will soon whisk passengers from small towns to the main lines of the transcontinental and world airways.

There has been considerable talk about the widespread use of the helicopter in postwar days. In spite of the great advances made in its development, it will probably be some time before its use becomes widespread. The helicopter itself can fly up, down, backward, frontward, and sidewise, but it is still difficult to fly unless its pilot has had considerable practice.

The helicopter gets its lift and its forward, backward, and sidewise movement from the big rotating blades above the fuselage. These blades have the same effect as those of a propeller. The big blades bite into the air as they turn. The shape of the blade is like the airfoil or wing of a plane. As it bites into the air it creates a lift just as a wing does. By the use of his controls the pilot can change the angle of the blades to increase or diminish their lift. For example, when the lift is reduced on a blade on one side of the plane it banks off in the direction of the reduced lift. The same holds true for any movement of the helicopter. A small rotor in a vertical position at the tail has controllable blades, and the machine is steered by changing the angle of these blades. The pilot of a helicopter of today is a very busy fellow. New developments, however, will probably simplify the operation of the machine.

The year 1945 marks the beginning of the forty-third year of powered flight in America. Before we celebrate the fiftieth anniversary of the first flight of the Wright Brothers at Kitty Hawk air travel will be the world's primary means of transportation. No spot on the globe will be more than fifty hours distant from wherever you may live. Truly the shortest distance between any two points on earth will be an airline!

During the last few years we have seen the airplane being developed into the mightiest weapon of war that the world has ever seen. We have witnessed the miracle of the creation of our great Army and Navy aërial task forces. And we have seen our air forces lead the way to victory over the enemies of our civilization. Just as the airplane brought us peace, it must also be retained as a military weapon that will always be a threatening force to restrain any fanatics who may again seek to destroy democracy and peace.

As a commercial transport, the airplane will also serve to keep the peace. Commercial airliners will make the world much smaller, and no nation will be a great distance from another. We shall all be able to travel by air to the most far-distant country in a matter of hours. All nations will be closer neighbors, and we shall all have a better understanding of our neighboring nations. The more we visit and mingle with the people of the entire world the more we can help to spread the doctrine of democracy of America. The airplane will play a great part in eliminating the greed and jealousy that breeds war. The young people of today will govern America tomorrow. The airplane will be the vehicle through which they will learn to know the peoples of the world. Through this better understanding America may always be the symbol of peace and prosperity.

However and wherever you fly, here's wishing you all "Happy Landings!"

♦ ♦ ♦

www.ingramcontent.com/pod-product-compliance
Ingram Content Group UK Ltd.
Pitfield, Milton Keynes, MK11 3LW, UK
UKHW041824200726
13854UKWH00002BA/533